Animal Antics

Animal Antics

INSPIRATIONAL STORIES, QUOTES, AND QUIPS ABOUT PETS AND ANIMALS

Mary Hollingsworth
GENERAL EDITOR

Guideposts Books
CARMEL, NEW YORK

Unless otherwise noted, all Scripture quotations are taken from *The Holy Bible, New Century Version®*, copyright © 1987, 1988, 1991 by Thomas Nelson, Inc. All rights reserved.

Scripture quotations marked ICB are from the *International Children's Bible.* Copyright © 1986, 1988 by Thomas Nelson, Inc. All rights reserved.

Editorial, research, and content development managed by Shady Oaks Studio, Bedford, Texas. Team members: Patty Crowley, Vicki Graham, Rhonda Hogan, Mary Hollingsworth, Laura Kendall, Mary Kay Knox, Kathryn Murray, Nancy Norris, Stephany Stevens, Stephanie Terry, and Barbara Tork.

Produced in association with Mark Sweeney & Associates, Bonita Springs, Florida.

www.guideposts.org
(800) 431-2344
Guideposts Books & Inspirational Media Division
Designed by Cindy LaBreacht
Cover by Lookout Design Group
Typeset by Inside Out Design & Typesetting

Printed in the United States of America

Contents

Introduction

Fuzzy and feisty, cuddly and cute—we're crazy about our pets and animals! They're our furry kids, and we adore them . . . just as they do us. We're family; it's just that simple. And woe to the person who tries to come between our pets and us!

Animals can be endearing, challenging, pesky, and precious. They're hilarious at times and the source of great joy. Their antics leave us rolling off the sofa or shaking our heads in disbelief. What would we do for entertainment if we didn't have them?

Animal Antics is a delightful collection of laughable incidents about pets and animals that will tickle your fancy and regale you with amazing, and sometimes ridiculous, events. And don't think this is just about cats and dogs either—we've got everything from hamster hilarity to some good old comical horse sense!

So sit down in your favorite chair and relax as we wander into the ever enjoyable animal kingdom . . . no wait! Fluffy needs to go for a walk first. Sigh.

Let There Be Laughter! is a series of books created with one purpose in mind—to brighten your spirit, lighten your load, and give you delightful moments of restorative laughter. We at

Guideposts assembled a team to look high and low for funny and wholesome writings that celebrate the lighter side of living. This series is the result of their research. And we hope you have as much fun reading it as they did putting it together.

You'll find stories relating hilarious, real-life tales; rib-tickling jokes and cartoons; absurd, frozen-moment-in-time anecdotes; top-ten lists and other miscellaneous grin-getters; great quotations that make you smile; and some of the best one-liners we've ever seen.

God gave us laughter! And believe it, He knew what He was doing. Because we wish you a dose of healthy fun and inspiration, we give you this book. In the midst of your day-to-day life, may it bring a smile to your face and true joy to your heart.

Let there be laughter!

The Editors

God created every living thing that moves in the sea . . .
He also made every bird that flies . . .
and He made the wild animals, the tame animals and
all the small crawling animals.
Genesis 1:21, 25 (ICB)

And he must have had a lot of fun doing it!

MARY HOLLINGSWORTH

1

Meow . . . Yeow!

"A dog is a dog, a bird is a bird, and a cat is a person," says Mugsy Peabody. There is something so righteous and arrogant about a cat that you just have to respect it. The rest of the time, it's a clown.

THE CAT WHO CAME BACK

I was foraging in the general store on my usual monthly run into town when a voice seemed to just barge into my thoughts: *Michael, why don't you pick up a few cans . . . just in case?* I was standing in front of a shelf full of cat food. *Just in case of what?* I wondered. Just in case that darn stray cat came sniffing around my place again? If I was going to do anything with a can of cat food I would probably throw it at him. I'd moved way out here in the middle of nowhere—a 12-mile truck drive, then six more miles via snowmobile from town—so no one would bother me.

But the urge to buy cat food kept at me. Finally I picked up

a few cans and shoved them in with the rest of my groceries.
I headed for the register.

I dreaded this part. I'd have to stand there while the girl
rang me up. Sure, she was used to me, never asked questions.
But it was uncomfortable standing there while she eyeballed
each and every item, like I was being x-rayed or something.
The cat food. That would get her attention.

I stared at the wall above her head, down at the floor, at
my hands.

"You got a cat?" she asked, her eyebrows arched as she
rang up the cans.

"Nope," I said. Her face red, she went back to bagging my
things without saying a another word. Probably thought I
was trying to stretch my food dollar.

I paid for my stuff, piled into my pickup and hit the long,
snowy road home. Home was a cabin I'd built myself, from
scratch, using money from a small inheritance and some of
my savings. My nearest neighbor—a real nice lady named
Ina Rae—was two miles away. Close enough.

If I sound like a fellow who'd given up on life, well, that's
not quite true. I'd given up on *people*. I suppose it started
when I was small. My parents were kind of rough on me. I'd
hide out in my room and stay below the radar. If this was the
way people who were supposed to love you treated you, then
just imagine how the rest of the world must be, animals
included. And God? Well, when you give up on people you
kind of give up on him too. I guess.

I graduated high school by the skin of my teeth. College?
Yeah, right. I hit the road and didn't look back. I hadn't talked
to my folks since. In fact, I didn't even know where they lived
anymore.

I worked a whole bunch of jobs, eventually settling in as a
janitor at a school. People left me alone unless something
needed fixing. I made sure things stayed fixed. Sometimes I'd

go down to the boiler room or into an empty classroom and read. One of my favorite books was *Walden* by Henry David Thoreau. Thoreau sought meaning by living alone in a cabin on a lake. That appealed to me. Self-discovery. No one to answer to. No one to talk to. Just me.

I traveled. Alaska, British Columbia, the Yukon, all over the Northwest. Eventually I got to Sandpoint, in northern Idaho, and decided to stick around for a while. Found myself a nice spot of land and built my own Walden. There was something in the air here, just a nice feeling. Peaceful.

There was nothing better than sitting out on the deck and kicking back. I'd look at the mountains, the clouds, and the pine trees until my mind got quiet and all I could hear was the babbling creek. Times like that it was almost like I just dissolved into the air.

There was something in the air here, just a nice feeling. Peaceful.

One cold day when the air froze your breath as soon as you exhaled, something under the picnic table caught my eye. A splash of gray against the winter white. I stooped over for a better look. A cat. "Shoo!" I yelled. The critter looked up at me. I stamped my foot and yelled again. The cat shot off the deck and disappeared.

How the heck did a little cat get out here in the middle of nowhere anyway? I wondered. Well, it wasn't my problem, and I wasn't taking in boarders.

All right, then. So how come I'd just bought cat food? I couldn't come up with an answer. I stopped the pickup and transferred everything into my snowmobile. Still had another six miles to go.

Yep, I really was in the middle of nowhere. Once in a while I'd run into Ina Rae. She knew not to ask me too many questions. *Maybe you could get her to come take the cat,* I thought.

The snowmobile bounced along, jarring me back to my

senses. *Get Ina Rae to take the cat? And then be caught up with her always telling you about how it's doing, asking if you want to visit? No way.*

It was bad enough I had to deal with people in town once a month.

I finally reached my cabin. No sign of the cat. I put away my provisions, shaking my head at myself for wasting good money on cat food.

Next morning, there he was, out on the deck. Just a ball of gray fur. He wasn't moving. I walked over. Was he dead? No. Still breathing. I couldn't just leave him out there. I cradled him close to my chest, carried him inside and sat down next to the stove. His fur was covered with ice. After a while he opened his eyes and stretched a bit. Then he reached a paw out toward me.

"Hey," I said, shaking it.

I set out the cat food in a bowl next to some water. He was wary at first, but when he finally dug in he practically licked the dish clean. I let him be while I did some chores. Frankly, I wondered how I'd ever get rid of him now. Then, just like that, he was gone. I felt panickly. "Here, cat!" I called from the deck. I went back in and searched all over. No cat.

Fine, I told myself. *Better that he doesn't start depending on you anyway.*

He came back, though, scratching at the door. That night he jumped up onto the bed and settled down on my pillow. "Get out of here! It's bad enough I took you in. You are not sleeping with me!" I nudged the cat off the bed. He jumped right back on. The only way I got any sleep was to give in and let him stay.

The next morning I decided that maybe Ina Rae could give me some advice.

"Michael, what a surprise!" she said when I showed up at her door.

"I found this cat," I told her, "and he's driving me nuts."

"Cats are all different," she told me. "But don't worry; he'll let you know what he needs. And he'll settle in eventually."

"He'd better not," I said. "Come spring, he's gone."

One morning I awoke to a quiet rumbling, like an outboard motor way off in the distance, as peaceful a sound as I'd ever heard. I lay back and just let it kind of vibrate through me, and for the first time in years I found myself thinking of my parents. Finally I turned my head. The cat was curled in a ball, eyes closed, purring contentedly.

"What am I gonna call you?" I asked him. "Can't keep saying 'cat' all the time." I went through a bunch of possibilities, finally settling on Jake.

Jake slept next to my head every night. He followed me on walks in the woods and nestled in my lap while I sat out on the deck. Ina Rae told me how happy I looked. Once she wouldn't have dreamed of saying such a thing.

Time for my monthly supply run came. I loaded up on cat food. The poor checkout girl probably thought I'd developed a taste for it. Taking a big breath, I gave her the news. "I got a cat. His name's Jake." It was the first time in a long time I'd told anyone a thing about myself. . . . Just a simple, insignificant fact, but for me it was a momentous occasion.

You know something? It felt good. It felt like I'd opened a window and let some fresh air in. And I found myself saying a little prayer. *Thanks, God, for sending me that little cat. You knew I needed someone like Jake. You knew it all along, I bet.* Now I was anxious to get home to my cat.

Plowing through the backwoods of Idaho on my snowmobile, I couldn't help but think of how beautiful everything looked, almost as if I hadn't noticed it before. I really did live an isolated existence. Even Thoreau eventually rejoined society. Maybe other people weren't so bad after all, at least in small doses. I mean, look how wrong I'd been about cats.

And while I was at it, maybe I could track down my folks and give them a ring.

Michael Sowders

• •

I have cats because they have no artificially imposed, culturally prescribed sense of decorum. They live in the moment. If I had an aneurysm in the brain and dropped dead, I love knowing that, as the paramedics carry me out my cats are going to be swatting at that little toe tag.

Paul Provenza

The cat and the love you give away come back to you.

Michael Hodgin

• •

INVISIBLE CAT

Whoever said, "Hell hath no fury like a woman scorned," was incorrect. Hell hath no fury like a cat that has to visit the veterinarian. This cliché was clearly demonstrated to me last week.

I was sitting at my computer at home on Saturday morning, still in my robe, drinking coffee and reading my email. It's Saturday, after all, why rush? My daughter came in: "Did you take the cat already?"

"Take the cat? Where? OH! NO!" I had 15 minutes to get dressed and get there. I had made the appointment a month ahead as Saturday appointments are so hard to get—how could I forget?

I jumped into jeans and a sweatshirt and grabbed the cat carrier. "Where is the cat?" How is it that animals seem to know when it is time to disappear? A frantic search under the beds, behind the furniture, and in the closets and garage finally produced a cat.

Trying to get a reluctant cat into the carrier would make a good comedy sketch. Somehow she became all legs and claws. She sprawled her legs, caught the edge of the door, twisted and fought frantically, and refused to get inside. I eventually managed to squeeze her in and convince her that she was going whether she liked it or not.

I thought she would scream all the way there, but actually she was pretty good considering that cats, unlike dogs, hate riding in the car. I turned on the radio as I've always heard that music soothes the savage beast. I'm not certain if that includes country music, but that's all I could find on the radio. She was strangely silent, however, pretending that she was not there, probably hoping that I would forget about her.

I sped to the vet's office, keeping an eye in the rear view mirror—not that I would exceed the speed limit, of course. I screeched into the parking lot, grabbed the cat carrier, and ran inside, only 5 minutes late.

"Is Frisky here for her shots?"

At about that moment, Frisky realized where she was and let out a blood-curdling howl that would have rivaled any of her wild, African cousins. Apparently, she recalled her last experience at the vet and had no intention of repeating it.

"It's only shots this time!" I told her. Of course, she didn't understand and continued to scream bloody murder as we were ushered into the examination room. For all the difficulty I had getting her in the carrier, you would think it would be easy to get her out. Are you kidding? She made herself as flat as possible at the back of the carrier and tried hard to become invisible. Finally, I had to drag her from the box. Her heart was pounding, and I knew she was scared to death.

I tried to calm her but her eyes remained wide and her heart rate fast. The vet came and did the necessary deed quickly. Frisky was now finished for a year. This time, I had no problem getting her back into the box where she again squeezed herself into the corner and tried to disappear.

We had a peaceful ride back home. Thank God for cat carriers. I could never have done it without one. The cat meowed some, but I think she was just complaining to me about taking her to that horrible place where innocent cats are jabbed with needles.

Back home, I opened the door to the carrier and she shot out like a bullet and ran to the back of the house and hid under the bed. I've not seen her since. I know she still lives here as her cat food is eaten and the litter box needs cleaning.

Apparently, she has finally accomplished her goal of becoming invisible.

Sheila Moss

"*We are not amused.*"

INTELLIGENT CAT

A rush and a dash and a scamper,
A warm, nestling armful of fur,
Our brief game of tag—being over—
Gave place to the tenderest purr.

He measures a yard in the morning
When stretched in a sweet, dreamless sleep,
The rich tawny fur, soft as velvet,
Showing broad, even stripes, dark and deep.

He lies on my lap in the sunshine;
I rock him to sleep on my arm;
I feel all the pleasure of loving
And striving to shield him from harm.

He runs up the tree to my window
To tap with his paw on the pane
And plead, in his sweet coaxing language,
For comfort and shelter again.

Each movement of gentle contentment,
Replete with luxurious grace,
Proclaims him at once and forever
The king of the feline race

Grace Bacon Holway

• •

A little girl is out in the backyard brushing the dog's teeth, and her father stops by and says, "What are you doing?" She says, "Well, I'm brushing Scuffy's teeth." She pauses and says to her father, "Don't worry, Dad. I'll put your toothbrush back like I always do."

Michael Hodgin

• •

TEMPORARY INSANITY

Maybe it was the big brown eyes that were to blame. Or perhaps it was the curly, non-shedding hair and turned up tail. Or it could have just been temporary insanity. Yes, temporary insanity was the reason I brought the dog home.

After twenty-five years of marriage I knew better than to bring home another pet without consulting my husband. I also knew it was best to pray before embarking on life changing decisions. I usually prayed at the drop of a hat, but I had neglected to do so before putting the dog in our car.

My mistake began when I read an email on the home-school message tree. "Due to allergies we must give away our beloved dog, Luis. He is a one-year-old labradoodle that loves children. He jumps through hoops, speaks, dances, plays dead, rolls over, and does other tricks."

Wow, I thought, *what a great dog*. Without stopping to think (never a good step) I picked up the phone. Like a dazed shopper racing for a limited supply of a much-desired item, adrenaline propelled me. "Can I come out and see him?" I asked.

Within minutes my four youngest kids and I were petting Luis who was very excited to meet us. We watched with delight at his cute tricks. By now, I had become the victim of a multiple personality. The sensible mother and wife, who shopped wisely and avoided impulsive behavior, gave way to the crazy dog lady. "We'll take him," the crazy lady announced. Before the transaction could be completed, the family wanted time to say good-bye to their dog.

I was scheduled to meet at a playground with three other moms so our kids could play together, so I told the mom that I would return in a couple of hours. I should have seized this "time-out" to regain my sanity. It was a missed opportunity for sure. Not until I was getting ready to leave the playground did I even admit to my friends that I was going to pick up a dog. My friends knew I already had two husband-approved dogs. So now you understand just how truly crazy the dog lady was.

I will forever be disappointed in my friends. Would they have let me reach for a third drink in the middle of the afternoon? I think not. Yet, they stood by and let me go for a third dog. Why didn't anyone slap me in the face and tell me to wake up? There were three of them. They could have formed a human shield and refused to let me leave the park. Instead, they did nothing but express surprise. "You are going to have three dogs?" one of them said, her eyes bugging out.

> **They could have formed a human shield and refused to let me leave the park.**

Even though I tried to ignore it, there was a small thin voice within me, trying to make contact. "What about your husband?" the voice asked.

"Oh, that's right," I thought. I called Mark at work. "Hi Mark. We're going to be taking care of a dog for another homeschooling family." A bit of small talk ensued and then I said good-bye. *There, took care of that,* I determined. It was actually the truth, sort of. Yeah, I know all about sins of omission. Guilty as charged.

If there was no difference in the mom's and one child's allergies with Luis gone, they wanted the dog back after two weeks. So I had convinced myself that we might not even keep him anyway. I'd let Mark in on the rest of the story after he realized how cute the dog was. Our own two dogs were getting old. They were happy to lie around all day, so one more dog would not really add much, I figured.

But when I walked in the door and looked at the three furry animals in my living room, I suddenly felt like a zookeeper. Three was way more than two. "Let's pick up the clutter and move this toy box upstairs so there's more room around here," I ordered, trying to stop the feeling that the walls were closing in.

One of the first things Luis began doing in his new home was barking loudly and often. Luis clearly had no affection for men, and mine is a male dominated household. We have eight boys (six still at home) and two girls. The two little boys were fine, but the older ones were teens, so Luis found them manly enough not to like. (You probably have noted that the crazy dog lady also has four teenagers.) Our house not only felt smaller, but noisier.

We put Luis in his indoor kennel that evening. He barked and howled all night. As I lay awake listening to the mournful howls, which pierced through my bedroom door, earplugs, and the hum of a fan, I had time to think. What had I done? I prayed about the situation finally. But what was I praying for? For God to vaporize Luis? For a time machine to go back and conduct myself appropriately? I prayed for God's will to be done, whatever that was concerning Luis.

By the next morning, Saturday, I confessed everything to Mark. He did not like the dog. The kids cried. Luis would stop howling at night and barking so much once he settled in, I reasoned. Mark had errands and I had a meeting to go to. I stopped at church and prayed before the tabernacle: "Your will be done, Lord."

Back at home, Mark said we could keep the dog. The kids were ecstatic. I was not sure what I thought anymore. Day after day, the kids played with and loved the dog. Night after night he howled. He was not warming up to the boys. Things always seem worse at night, and that is when remorse overwhelmed me. *Why had I been so stupid?* I asked myself listening to the howls. *I had been greedy to grab a dog I thought everyone else would want. I had been inconsiderate to my husband. I had neglected to pray first and now I was paying.*

After several nights, I let Luis sleep with the girls. This made him happy and quiet at least at night. Then, the beginning of the end appeared under our dining room table. That's where he pooped. Years of diapers are one thing but loose poop in the house is another. My daughters excused it stating he was probably whimpering to go out but they had not paid attention. Then, the next day, it happened again. It was then that I knew what I had to do—repent of my sin and return the dog.

I emailed the dog's owners late Saturday evening (minutes after finding poop #2) and explained the dog was not working out. Sunday morning (we had gone to Mass Saturday evening), I took six of the kids fishing. Mark stayed home with two of the teenagers and slept in. I had to bring Luis with us so he would not howl and wake them up or poop in the house. It was this fishing trip that insured that the kids would not miss Luis. We tied him up very close to us, so he could see us fish. But Luis howled and barked because he wanted to be with us among the poles, hooks and tackle. He made a nuisance of himself all morning. By the time we returned home, Luis's owner had called to say he would come by and take him back. My kids realized he would ruin our lives if he stayed. They were suddenly happy to see him go.

His original family had missed him and thought that maybe frequent baths could help alleviate any contribution he was making to their allergies. I apologized for the inconvenience I had caused. Then, when they drove away, I felt like doing cartwheels through the house. The mistake born of my temporary insanity was gone! The burden had lifted! Mark shared with me that he knew if he sent the dog away, the kids would think he was the bad guy. Yet, he did not want the dog. It seemed a no-win situation so he put it to prayer. Mark trusted that God would handle it.

Not working in union with God and my spouse had proved disastrous. God can use all things for good and I think this whole incident served as an example to my kids. They saw what happens when one acts alone without God's guidance and the difference when one puts a situation to prayer and trusts God to work it out. It's no fun serving as the bad example, so I will try to avoid that role in the future. I am confident we have seen the last of the crazy dog lady.

Patti Armstrong

••

I looked at all the caged animals in the shelter . . . the cast-offs of human society.

I saw in their eyes love and hope, fear and dread, sadness and betrayal.

And I was angry.

"God, I said, "this is terrible!

Why don't you do something?"

God was silent for a moment and then He spoke softly.

"I have done something," He replied.

"I created YOU."

Jim Willis

Our cat became the proud mama to five kittens. After determining they were all male, I looked at them and said, "What shall we name you?" Without missing a beat, my husband replied, "Matthew, Mark, Luke, John, and Ralph."

Stevie Stevens

••

THE DOG (AS SEEN BY THE CAT)

The Dog is black or white or brown
And sometimes spotted like a clown.
He loves to make a foolish noise,
And Human Company enjoys

The Human People pat his head
And teach him to pretend he's dead.
And beg, and fetch, and carry, too;
Things that no well-bred Cat will do.

At Human jokes, however stale,
He jumps about and wags his tail,
And Human People clap their hands
And think he really understands.

They say "Good Dog" to him. To us
They say "Poor Puss" and make no fuss.
Why Dogs are "good" and Cats are "poor"
I fail to understand, I'm sure.

To Someone very Good and just
Who had proved worthy of her trust,
A Cat will sometimes condescend—
The dog is everybody's friend!

Oliver Herford

A CAT'S HEAVEN

St. Peter is standing at heaven's pearly gates when a cat
shows up. "You were a loving cat on earth," says St. Peter,

"so I want to give you one special thing you have always wanted."

"Well, I did always want a nice satin pillow like my master had, so I could lie on it."

"That's easy," St. Peter replied. "We will have a satin pillow ready for you."

Next a family of mice appears at the pearly gates.

St. Peter says, "Ah, I remember you. You were good mice on earth. You didn't steal food from anyone's house and never hurt other animals. Therefore, I want to grant you one special wish."

The father mouse replied, "Well, we always watched the children skating, and it looked like fun. Could we each have some skates, please?"

"Granted. You shall have your wish."

The next day, St. Peter saw the cat sunning itself on the pillow. "Well, cat, how's the satin pillow?"

"Absolutely wonderful," the cat replied. "And say, those 'Meals on Wheels' were an extra nice touch too!"

Jim Kraus

"A Nigerian prince wants to send me 10 million dead mice!"

••

If man could be crossed with the cat, it would improve the man but deteriorate the cat.

Mark Twain

••

'FRAIDY CAT

We got her at the place for friendless or abandoned animals—a tiny gray-and-white kitten whose eyes were still blue. Just an alley cat, nameless, homeless, too young to lap milk from a saucer—we had to feed her with an eye-dropper. She didn't like the strange new world in which she found herself. She hid under the bed and cried. We laughed and called her Fraidy Cat.

She soon got used to us, of course. She slept a lot and played games with balls of wadded paper. I never saw her chase her tail, as kittens are supposed to do. But she had a good time.

She had an even better time when we moved to the country. She was half-grown then and liked to stalk things in the tall grass behind the house. Twice she brought home a mouse for us to admire, and once, a bird. Fortunately the bird wasn't hurt, so we took it away from her and let it go. She seemed to think our distinction between mice and birds was pretty silly. Logically, she was right.

She was an aloof little beast in those days—I say "little" because she remained a very small cat. She didn't show much affection for anyone. In fact, if you tried to pet her when she wasn't in the mood, she would dig her claws in harder than was pleasant or even bite. This didn't bother me, of course, because I am really a dog man. I can take cats or leave them alone.

We acquired a dog soon after we moved to the country, a

friendly boxer named Major. Fraidy loathed him. For the first month or so, if he came too close, she would spit and rake his nose, leaving him hurt and bewildered. I was rather indignant about this—after all, I'm a dog man—and I slapped Fraidy once or twice for assaulting Major. "Who do you think you are?" I asked her. "Try to remember you're nothing but a cat!"

While she was still too young, in our opinion, for such goings-on, Fraidy decided to become a mother. When the time came, however, she didn't hide away like most cats; she stuck close to us. Maybe she had a hunch it was going to be tough. It was. There was only a single kitten, much too big. She couldn't handle it herself; I had to help her. It took all my strength, and I thought she would bite me, but she didn't. She just watched me, her yellow eyes glassy with pain. Afterward, she licked my hand. But the kitten was born dead.

"Never mind, Fraidy," we said. "You'll have better luck next time."

For days she was gaunt and thin; she looked for the kitten everywhere. I believe she thought Major was responsible for its disappearance—all her old distrust of him came back, for a while. She got over that, but one thing she did not get over: her gratitude to me. She followed me from room to room, and if I sat down she would jump into my lap, put her forefeet on my chest, and stare into my face with the most soulful look imaginable.

"Typical woman," my wife said, laughing. "In love with her obstetrician."

"It's just misplaced maternal instinct," I said. "She'll get over it as soon as she has some kittens."

Nature, it seemed, had the same idea, because before very long Fraidy was pregnant again. We figured she would have at least two kittens, this time. Smaller ones. We were very happy for her. She seemed sleepy and satisfied.

Then one day, not long ago, she developed a cough. We thought nothing of it; her appetite was good. She seemed somewhat lethargic, but after all, her time was almost due. Then, early yesterday morning, she came up from the kitchen where she slept and jumped on our bed. She curled up in my lap and looked at me. She meowed unhappily.

"What's the matter with this fool cat?" I said. "What's she trying to tell us?"

All yesterday she didn't eat. She even refused water. In the evening, finally, I called a vet. There are good vets, I guess, and bad ones. This one—when he saw her—said it seemed to be just a cold. No fever. Nothing very wrong. That was yesterday.

This morning Fraidy Cat dragged herself upstairs again, but this time she couldn't jump onto the bed. She was too weak. The roof of her mouth was very pale; her eyes were glazed.

I telephoned another vet. It was Sunday morning, and early, but he said to bring her over. I did. He examined her carefully. He knew his business; you can always tell.

"I'm sorry," he said. "Uterine infection. I'm afraid the kittens are dead."

"Can't you operate?" I said. "Can't you save her?"

He shook his head. "I could try. But it would just prolong things. She's pretty far gone now." He looked at my face. He was a kind man, and he loved animals. "I'd put her away," he said gently, "if I were you."

After a while I nodded my head.

"Now?" said the vet, "or after you've gone?"

"I'll stay with her," I said.

He brought the hypodermic needle and the Nembutal. "It doesn't hurt," he said. "She'll go to sleep, that's all." The needle went home, quick and merciful.

She was just an ordinary alley cat. She had no pedigree, no clever tricks. But I remembered how she'd roll over on the path when we'd drive up in the car. I remembered how she loved to eat slivers of melon from our breakfast plates. I remembered

> She was just an ordinary alley cat. She had no pedigree, no clever tricks.

how she liked to have her ears scratched, and how she licked my hand the day I had to hurt her so terribly, the day her kitten was born dead.

I stood there with my hand touching her so that perhaps she would not be afraid. "It's all right, Fraidy," I said. "Go to sleep. Go to sleep." And at last she put her head down on her clean little paws and closed her eyes.

I felt blindly for my pocketbook. It wasn't there. "I haven't any money," I said. "I'll have to send it to you."

"That's all right," the vet said. "Don't bother."

I touched her ear for the last time and turned back to the door. It was a golden summer morning, calm, serene. Down in the meadow a gigantic willow tree made a burst of greenness against the sky.

I got in the car quickly and drove away. But not far down the road I stopped the car and put my forehead against the steering wheel and wept. Because she was such a little cat. Because she had tried to tell me that she was sick, that she was in trouble, and I hadn't helped her. Not until too late. And I felt the awful emptiness that comes from not knowing how much you love something until you have lost it.

Arthur Gordon

off the mark.com
by Mark Parisi
PRE-RINSE CYCLE
ATLANTIC FEATURE ©1999 MARK PARISI
offthemark.com
MARK PARISI

2

"Dog" Spelled Backward Is "God"

And for dog lovers, that's altogether appropriate. They are delightful, demanding, and sometimes totally demented, it seems. They make us laugh, they make us cry, and they steal our hearts.

PRINCESS FUR-FACE

"What'ya say we change the furniture around?" Ken queried one Saturday morning as we were finishing our last cups of coffee/tea. "Let's put the couch by the window and the two chairs facing the fireplace." I had learned years before to trust Ken's fine eye for furniture placement.

"Sounds good to me, Babe," I said, "but do you have the stamina for Ashley's neurotic response?"

Ashley was our cocker spaniel who reacted strongly against all visual changes. She wanted things to remain in their accustomed spots. If they didn't, she had one of her "spells." It didn't matter how big or small the change; each warranted a protest. Let me give you an example.

A friend popped in on me one morning and for some reason just dropped her purse in the middle of the floor as we made our way to the "chat chairs" by the window. (This was before the rearrangement.) Several moments later Ashley, who hated to miss anything, came trotting into the room. Spotting my friend's purse in the middle of the floor, she skidded to a stiff-legged halt, stared briefly at the purse, and went into a dramatic fit of barking. Slowly circling the purse, she barked, growled, and scowled until my friend finally placed her purse behind the chair. Gradually Ashley settled down, but it was obvious the visit was ruined for her.

As Ken pondered the price to be paid for furniture rearrangement, he noted that Ashley was out on the deck dozing in the sun. She might not notice what was going on until the dastardly deed was done.

Several hours later Ashley roused herself from her siesta and ambled into the house. She immediately assessed that unauthorized changes had occurred in her absence. After barking herself nearly hoarse, she flounced out of the living room and stayed in her "sleep area" for several days. We delivered her food and water. Gradually she came to realize that the couch was now in a far better spot for her because she was able to see out the window. (Of course she was allowed on the furniture!) This made it possible for her to visually patrol the neighborhood without leaving the comforts of home.

Perhaps the greatest trauma Princess Fur-Face had to endure was when we got a new car.

Perhaps the greatest trauma Princess Fur-Face had to endure was when we got a new car. Ashley's sleep area was in a small room adjoining the garage, and although the car wasn't fully visible to her, it was in close proximity.

On the first night of their cohabitation, Ashley,

who had not yet been introduced to the new car, scampered down the stairs to bed as was her custom. We stood behind the closed door holding our breath. No sound . . . no barking . . . no response at all. Ken's theory was that because it was dark, Ashley couldn't see the car. Our intention was to later, in the daylight, gradually coax her into an accepting relationship with the new vehicle.

Around 1 A.M. we were awakened by the sound of frantic, ferocious barking. Ashley had discovered the car. Fearing she'd disturb the neighbors, Ken flew down the stairs, scooped up Ashley along with her bed, and deposited her in our room, something Ken normally refused to do. She grumbled and complained the rest of the night, but at least she didn't bark.

Because Ken drove the car to work during the day, I had no opportunity to ease Ashley into a spirit of charitableness about the car. Each night she seemed to forget about the alien in the garage when she first went to bed, then rediscover it sometime after midnight.

At 2 A.M. on the fourth night of Ashley's histrionics, Ken exasperatedly dragged himself out of bed and announced he had just come up with a plan which required we both get dressed and take Ashley for a ride.

"Are you going to dump her out of the car somewhere in another county?" I asked cautiously as I threw on jeans and a sweatshirt.

"Trust me" was all he said.

Ken thrust a squirming, growling, barking cocker into my arms, and we got in the monster car to begin what Ken said would be the "taming ride." For at least an hour Ashley was a bundle of growling rigidity in my arms. With the radio playing soft music and both of us stroking Ashley with words of love and encouragement (none of which we felt at that moment), Ashley began to relax. An hour and a half later and miles from home, she went limp in my arms and fell asleep. From that moment on, Ashley had peace about her metal roommate. In fact, one of her favorite activities became riding in the car.

I hate to tell you how closely I identify with Ashley at times. There are God-gifts I have fought so fervently only to find that once I yield my resisting spirit I reap incredible benefits. For example, I certainly don't overly resist the concept of grace, but I've tried to earn it a million times. I seem to tenaciously cling to the mistaken notion that I've got to be good enough in order to deserve grace. How many times does God have to hold my rigidly resisting spirit until finally, with celestial music in my ears, I relax and embrace his gift?

Ashley learned with just one ride.

Marilyn Meberg

ZORRO

Zorro the new puppy is here. My daughter's dog looks like a miniature blue heeler, and he fits in the palm of my hand.

He doesn't know he's a little dog. He's 100 percent puppy, with all the chewing, jumping, leaping, eating, and tinkling that indicates. He has the attention span of a gnat, plays until he crashes, and makes us frustrated and laugh all in the same breath.

In short, he's like a toddler.

I'd almost forgotten what it was like to have a little one in the house again. Almost. See, this morning I was on my couch during my study and prayer time, trying to get quiet before the day unfolded. Hot coffee, fresh pen, and a still house after the children left for school. A perfect opportunity.

And then came Zorro. Cavorting on my lap. Chewing on my pen. Gnawing the corners of my cozy throw blanket.

David the psalmist wrote, "His delight is in the law of the Lord, and in His law he meditates day and night."

It's hard to meditate when a half-pound dog is wriggling with all his might, hoping to get a good lick at your ear.

I actually prayed God would make Zorro quiet so I could focus.

Didn't happen.

It reminded me of when my children were small, when I longed to pursue deeper spirituality, but there wasn't enough time, or frankly, enough energy.

Babies are time consuming, and can be mentally and physically exhausting. It seemed every time I found stillness, instead of praying, I'd be asleep.

My season has changed, but God sends me reminders. Zorro, the toddler Chihuahua. I close my book and pick up this little fuzzball of love and nuzzle his baby face.

I remember.

Britta Coleman

. . . .

Outside of a dog, a book is a man's best friend. Inside a dog, it's too dark to read.

Groucho Marx

An Easterner walked into a Western saloon and saw a dog sitting at a table playing poker with three men. He asked, "Can that dog really play cards?" One of the men answered, "Yeah, but he ain't much of a player. Whenever he gets a good hand he wags his tail."

Michael Hodgin

. . . .

"The leftovers sound good."

STONEY COMES HOME

When I first saw Stoney, he whisked across the room like a silver rocket at warp speed. Orbiting twice, he landed in my lap and nestled his face beneath my chin. I was smitten!

Due to an illness in the family, friends giving up this white and gray llasa Apso believed Stoney and I were perfect for each other.

"This dog is smart, cute, and soft as an 18-pound cotton ball," they promised. "He is perfect for you!"

"I don't know," I hesitated. "I travel a lot these days and . . ."

"He's housebroken."

"So when can I get him?"

My heart melted when I met him and we quickly became best buddies. He shadows my every move. When I climbed into bed that first night, Stoney stared with big heart-tugging black eyes that said, "That bed sure looks nice." I scooped him up and giggled as he circled several times then snuggled against my back, sighed, and quickly began a gentle snore.

I was happy to discover that, like me, Stoney doesn't DO mornings! He has an industrial-sized bladder and it is 10:00 a.m. or so before he feels the need to go outside and . . . well, you know.

This precious pup has changed my life. I feel wholly loved. Stony reminds me to play by dropping a toy at my foot and rubbing against my leg. He sits beside me on the sofa, reminding me that cuddling is a wonderful thing. When I come home, he greets me with jumps and a spirited dance. When he needs to go outside and . . . well, you know, he barks and runs toward his leash. Some days we traverse the whole neighborhood as my discriminating dog determines where to deposit his DNA. But the exercise is healthy, plus I'm forging new friendships with neighbors who are attracted to this furry people magnet.

Stoney is love, and love is always to be cherished.

Still, the next time I pray for a loving, cuddly male to share my life, I should probably be a little more specific!

Cathy Lee Phillips

Bow-Wow . . . or Wang-Wang?

It's a truism we all learn as kids: A dog goes bow-wow . . . a cat goes meow . . . etc. A universal language, right? Nope. Believe it or not, animal sounds vary from language to language. Here are some examples.

PIGS
English: Oink Oink!
Russian: Kroo!
French: Groin Groin!
German: Grunz!

ROOSTERS
English: Cock-a-doodle-doo!
Arabic: Ku-ku-ku-ku!
Russian: Ku-ka-rzhi-ku!
Japanese: Ko-ki-koko!
Greek: Ki-ki-ri-koo!
Hebrew: Ku-ku-ri-koo!

DUCKS
English: Quack Quack!
Swedish: Kvack Kvack!
Arabic: Kack-kack-kack!
Chinese: Ga-ga!
French: Quahn Quahn!

FROGS
English: Croak!
Spanish: Croack!
German: Quak-quak!
Swedish: Kouack!
Russian: Kva-kva!

TWEETY-BIRDS
English: Tweet tweet!
French: Kwi-kwi!
Hebrew: Tsef Tsef!
Chinese: Chu-chu!
German: Tschiep Tschiep!

GEESE
English: Honk Honk!
Arabic: Wack Wack!
German: Schnatter-Schnatter!
Japanese: Boo Boo!

OWLS
  English: Who-whoo!
  Japanese: Ho-ho!
  German: Koh-koh-a-oh!
  Russian: Ookh!

CATS
  English: Meow!
  Hebrew: Miyau!
  French: Miaou!
  Spanish (and Portuguese and German): Miau!

DOGS
  English: Bow-wow!
  Swedish: Voff Voff!
  Hebrew: Hav Hav!
  Chinese: Wang-wang!
  Japanese: Won-won!
  Swahili: Hu Hu Hu Huuu!

CHICKENS
  English: Cluck-cluck!
  French: Cot-cot-cot-codet!
  German: Gak-gak!
  Hebrew: Pak-pak-pak!
  Arabic: Kakakakakakakakaka!

The Best of Uncle John's Bathroom Reader

• •

Did you ever walk in a room and forget why you walked in? I think that's how dogs spend their lives.

Sue Murphy

• •

THE TUMMY TIMER

My little Shih Tzu named Jazz has an automatic tummy timer. You can literally set your clock by this little blonde fifteen-pound ball of energy. At eight o'clock in the morning he gently sticks his nose in my ear to get me to wake up. He's hungry! And he wants me to get up and fix his breakfast. It doesn't matter what time we went to bed, at eight he's ready to eat. So he runs around in circles growling and woofing in anticipation while I put on my house shoes and robe. He's throwing his toy in the air and then chomping on it to make it squeak. At last we go downstairs where we're met by his adopted twin-like brother, Samson.

After breakfast and a romp in the backyard, Jazz spends most of the day in my office with me. He sleeps on the window seat or in a chair, and I rarely hear anything out of him until five o'clock that afternoon . . . that is unless he detects someone at the front door and feels compelled to act as my noisy, furry doorbell.

I don't have to worry about losing track of the time, though, because at straight up five o'clock Jazz starts whining and barking for me to stop what I'm doing and prepare his dinner. If I don't move quite as fast as he wants me to, he stands up on his hind legs and puts his front paws on my leg, nuzzling my arm with his nose and looking at me with his can't-you-see-that-I'm-dying-of-starvation chocolate-drop eyes. If that doesn't do the trick, he enlists Samson to help him bark. So I finally give in and go downstairs to fix their meal. (Jazz knows I will, of course; he has me very well trained. This gives a whole new meaning to the phrase "dog obedience school.")

After dinner and his evening constitutional, we usually play ball for a few minutes; then he flops down on my sheepskin rug and goes back to sleep. (It's a dog's life.)

Promptly at nine o'clock he wakes up out of a dead sleep, stretches as only a dog can do, and starts the whining-and-barking routine again. It's time for treats! It's absolutely uncanny how he knows what time it is, even when he's asleep. He literally starts this routine every single night within a three-minute time period on either side of nine-o'clock. And don't even *think* about trying to ignore him while you watch the beginning of a favorite television show, because you'll just be setting yourself up for an ear-splitting, level-nine canine chorus.

Most people worry about their electric alarm clocks going off in the middle of the night and their being late for work. I never have to worry about that—I have Jazz and his ever-accurate tummy timer!

Mary Hollingsworth

· ·

A press agent set up an audition with a famous television producer for his client, a talking dog. The skeptical producer warmed up as the dog started with a couple of jokes, then followed with an amusing political satire. The press agent explained that his client's real desire was to be a singer. After hearing the dog perform several songs, the producer was convinced he had found a gold mine. Suddenly, a huge, ugly dog burst into the audition studio, snatched up the little dog by the neck and dashed out the room. The producer was beside himself and turned to the press agent, who was putting on his coat to leave.

"What in the world happened?" the producer asked.

"That was his mother," the press agent answered dejectedly. "She wants him to be a doctor."

Tal D. Bonham

"He pretended to throw the ball, but he faked me out! It was the most humiliating experience of my life. Now I'm learning to live with the pain, one day at a time."

Dog Dictionary

Bicycles: Two-wheeled exercise machines, invented for dogs to control body fat. To get maximum aerobic benefit, hide behind a bush. When you spot one, dash out, bark loudly, and run alongside for a few yards. The human on the bike will swerve and fall into the bushes.

Deafness: This malady kicks in when your human calls. Symptoms include either running in the opposite direction or simply lying down.

Thunder: This is a signal that the world is coming to an end. Humans remain amazingly calm during thunderstorms, so it is necessary to warn them of the danger by trembling uncontrollably, panting, rolling your eyes wildly, whimpering or barking incessantly, and never letting them out of your sight.

Wastebasket: This is a doggie treasure chest regularly stocked with a changing array of interesting things. When you get bored, turn the basket over and strew the contents all over the house. When your human comes home, they're sure to express their excitement with your creative decorating.

Bath: This is a process by which humans drench the floor, walls, and themselves with your help. For added fun, shake vigorously and frequently.

Bump: The best way to get your human's attention when they are drinking a hot cup of coffee or tea.

Goose bump: A last-resort maneuver to use when the Bump doesn't get the attention you require.

Lean: Every good dog's response to the command "Sit," especially if your human is dressed for an evening out. Incredibly effective before black-tie events. Your hair adds a personal touch to the outfit.

Love: A feeling of intense affection, given freely and without restriction. Show your love by wagging your tail and giving slobbery kisses. If you're lucky, a human will love you in return.

Sofas: This is your doggie napkin. After eating, it is polite to run up and down the front of the sofa and wipe your face clean.

Dog bed: Any soft, clean surface, such as the white bedspread in the guest room or the newly upholstered couch in the living room.

Drool: What you do when your human has food and you

don't. To do this properly, you must sit as close as you can, look sad, and let the drool fall on their shoes, or better yet, on their lap.

Garbage can: An aromatic container that your neighbors put out once a week to test your ingenuity. Stand on your hind legs and push the lid off. If you do it right, you are rewarded with paper to shred, bones to consume, and stale pieces of bread to scatter throughout the neighborhood.

Leash: A strap that attaches to your collar, enabling you to lead your human everywhere you want him or her to go.

Jim Kraus

BLUE DOG

My dog is depressed. She lies under the grand piano with her tobacco-juice eyes closed. Won't even get up when I open a package of wieners, dragging out the tearing of the plastic wrap until all the crackling I am making sounds as if I am setting a fire. But there is no fire in her, not even to get up and investigate. When I hold the wieners in front of a fan to blow the smell toward her—nope—she just lies there, flat, like a rug or an Egyptian sphinx.

What started all of this was when my last child got his driver's license. No more carpools. My dog and I have been taken off the streets. We are home every day now from two to six. For a while we watched *Oprah*, and then we'd go out and dig in the dirt around my house.

But my dog doesn't much care about *Oprah*, and not much more about the dirt. Giving up my carpooling has saddened her.

All those years she went with me to drop the kids off—first in the morning early, when I didn't look good or feel sweet— she'd sit in the back seat of my station wagon and fog up the windows while snapping her teeth. She'd terrify the drivers in the next lane so we could jockey in position to beat the bell. At 2:00 p.m. she'd wait by the back door to go again to pick the kids up. Just the sound of my taking the car keys out of my purse could make her do a tap dance like she had hot feet on the kitchen floor.

From the back seat of my station wagon, she'd hang her head out of the window and let her tongue trail. She is a big mean-looking dog, the kind that men in pick-up trucks with rifles in their back windows admire at red lights. It's not uncommon to have them roll down their windows and get her riled up by making faces at her and then call out to me, "Nice dog, lady."

She's gone to piano lessons and waited at the curb; she likes country music on the radio. She's gone to and come back from soccer practices, Halloween carnivals, and Boy Scout meetings.

Now that she's taken up her down-in-the-mouth spot under the grand piano, I am tempted to pick up the car keys and jiggle them, just to see if she is all right. But that seems cruel. So I have started wrapping the keys in a paper towel so they can be picked up in silence. Because there is nowhere that I go now that I do not park, get out, and stay awhile.

It's a sad event—to just up and change a dog's life with no good warning. She had no way to know that those little kids who played with her as a puppy would one day get cars of their own. Then go on, grow up, and move all the way out.

Yesterday, I felt so sorry for her that I picked up the keys and let her do her hot pepper dance, then headed on out to the car. We've traded in the station wagon. We have a sedan now. And I let her sit beside me in the front seat. As we drove out of the driveway, her big hairy head came on over and rested on my arm near the gear shift.

We made a loop out to the soccer field, then to the piano teacher's where we parked by the curb and listened to the radio. Then we spun on out to the school, even though it was closed. On the way home, I drove her through Burger King and ordered her a Whopper, all the way, but told them to hold the pickles and onions.

Next Sunday I plan to drive her around again. It seems the only decent thing to do for a blue dog.

Shelley Fraser Mickle

Things I Learned from My Dog

Carpet is an unnecessary evil.

Throw-up on your bed is OK, as long as it's not where you sleep.

A lick/kiss on the face is one thing; a lick/kiss on the mouth is another altogether.

It's OK to pass gas whenever, wherever, and in front of whomever.

Odor Eaters replace shoe insoles quite nicely.

Walls can be patched.

Hanging drywall is easy.

Stuffed animals were not meant to be stuffed.

Let the mud dry on the carpet before you vacuum.

I can be gone less than a minute or ten hours, and I'll receive the same excited welcome.

My dog is smarter than most people I know.

I like my dog better than most people I know.

Lise-Ann Davis

....

A certain announcement appeared in the bulletin of a church in Sarasota, Florida: *"The Magic of Lassie*, a film for the whole family, will be shown Sunday at 5 p.m. in the church hall. Free puppies will be given to all children not accompanied by parents."

Michael Hodgin

I wonder if other dogs think poodles are members of a weird religious cult.

Rita Rudner

....

NATURAL-BORN ENEMIES

Charlie and I seemed meant for each other. He was a doctor, I was a nurse. We'd both lived in Germany and loved to speak the language. I had only one concern. My cat, Psyche, was like family to me. If Charlie was going to be part of my life, he had to love her too. Could he, and remain loyal to his beloved fawn-colored boxer, Kaiserene? "I'm willing to try," he said when I posed the dilemma.

It didn't take long for Psyche to turn Charlie into a cat person—or at least half a cat person. And when she wove an eight around his legs, that sealed the deal for me. "You must really be something special," I told him. "Psyche only does that to a true friend."

Charlie's dog won me over when she climbed up beside me on the couch and put her head in my lap. "I would love to have a dog like you," I said.

I got my wish when Charlie and I married. Psyche and I moved into his place, set on three and a half acres of woodland.

"You really landed in the cream," I told Psyche as I carried her up the front steps on moving day. I stepped inside and put her down to explore. Charlie put his arms around me. "Now everything's purrrfect," he said.

Just then we heard a low growl and a hiss. We ran into the living room. There was a face-off on the carpet. Psyche's back was arched. Kaiserene bristled all over and bared her teeth.

"Psyche!" I cried.

"Kaiserene, no!" called Charlie.

I took the cat in my arms. Charlie grabbed the dog by the collar.

"I don't think they like each other," Charlie said. That was an understatement. Charlie and I broke up their squabbles all over the house. One evening Kaiserene came across Psyche napping on the rug in the foyer. Psyche jumped up hissing. Kaiserene growled back. Before I could stop her, Psyche swiped at the dog's nose. Kaiserene yelped and Charlie pulled her into the living room.

I took Psyche to the bedroom and stroked her fur. "I'm sorry I brought you here," I said. When Psyche was calm I went back to the living room. Kaiserene lay on the floor, miserable. I helped Charlie clean her scraped nose. "I'm sorry I brought a cat into your house," I said. Kaiserene trembled and licked my hand.

"They'll never make nice," I told Charlie. "We've put natural-born enemies under the same roof."

After that episode, Psyche and Kaiserene called an uneasy truce. It made me sad. I wished they would do more than just tolerate each other.

One morning, about six months into our marriage, I let Psyche out our front door. Kaiserene was up on the neighbor's hill keeping watch on the yard. She didn't even look at Psyche darting around after a dragonfly. God, if these animals have guardian angels, do you think they could convince their furry charges to give each other another chance?

I was about to shut the door when I heard loud barking. Six stray dogs barreled into the yard. Psyche screeched. The pack chased her. She jumped into a holly bush. The menacing dogs had her surrounded! I ran outside. I had to save Psyche. Just then a fawn-colored streak raced down the hill—Kaiserene!

She leapt right into the middle of the dog pack, snarling and bristling. With her hair standing on end she looked twice her normal size. The sinister dogs stood their ground for only a moment, then ran away. Kaiserene chased them and barked until they were out of sight.

Kaiserene snorted. She loped over to the holly bush and cocked her head inquisitively. "Meow," I heard from the upper branches. Psyche picked her way down to the ground and looked up at the big, muscular dog towering over her. Oh, please don't let her take her fear out on this dog who just saved her!

"It's okay, Psyche," I said soothingly. But she ignored my voice. Instead she wove a figure eight through Kaiserene's front legs, purring and rubbing her head against the dog's wide chest. Kaiserene bent down and licked Psyche on the head. Then Kaiserene headed back to the hill to keep watch. Psyche went on with her frolicking.

I stood staring in shock. "Charlie," I called, "you're not going to believe this." Only angels could have orchestrated this new friendship between two animals who fought like, well, cats and dogs.

Juanzetta Flowers

• •

How many are your works, O Lord! In wisdom you made them all; the earth is full of your creatures.

Psalm 104:24

• •

"Essentially, I'm the child you never had. Since you won't be sending anyone to college, can I have the cash?"

10 Observations for Visitors Who Complain about My Pet

My pet lives here. You don't.

If you don't want his hair on your clothes, stay off the furniture. (Why do you think they call it "fur"niture?)

I like my pet a lot better than I like most people. So, watch it!

To you, my pet is an animal. To me, my pet is an adopted child, who happens to be short, hairy, and walks on all fours. (Nobody is perfect!) Although he doesn't speak English, he communicates with me extremely well. We understand each other . . . which is more than I can say for most people I know.

Don't feel bad, my pet growls at me too. He doesn't bite me, but as for you . . .

My pet kills spiders, mice, roaches, and other unwanted vermin for me. What can you do to help me?

When I come home, my pet is always excited to see me. He bounds around the room with glee, barks wildly, wags his tail, and brings me a toy to show how thrilled he is that I'm home. When was the last time you demonstrated your happiness to see me?

My pet is happy to eat leftovers—even slightly furry ones. You, on the other hand, expect me to cook. Duh!

My pet goes outside to use the bathroom. I never have to clean a toilet after him. But are you that considerate? Noooo. You insist on going inside the house. You don't even put the seat down, Sweetie!

In summary, dogs and cats are better than kids. They eat less, don't ask for money all the time, are easier to train, usually come when called (this does not apply to cats), never drive your car, don't hang out with drug-using friends, don't smoke or drink, don't worry about having to buy the latest fashions, don't wear your clothes, and don't need a jillion dollars for college. Also, if they get pregnant, you can sell the children!

A. Nony Mous
Expanded by Mary Hollingsworth

••

Teach your children to brush their teeth, brush their hair, and brush the dog. But not with the same brush. The dog resents it.

Author Unknown

••

JUST HOP ON MY BACK

The year my husband broke his arm, I had to take a crash course in animal husbandry. Up until that time, I had always thought animal husbandry meant learning how to deal with a cantankerous husband. But by the time Len was back full-steam, I knew what it really meant.

I did, however, discover that there really isn't that much difference between taking care of farm animals and taking care of a husband and kids. You feed and water them; you keep their living quarters shoveled out—and that's about the same thing you do for your farm animals.

There was one thing more I learned during this time: the fine art of mountain climbing. Now, my mountain was only eight feet high, but it might as well have been eight hundred feet high. And I didn't climb it "because it was there": I climbed it because *I* was there.

It was the day I brought Len home from the hospital. Those dirt roads were packed with ice and incredibly slick. I wasn't used to driving on them because before Len broke his arm, he always did the driving when it was icy. I did a lot of "backseat" driving, but believe me, the view is a lot different from the driver's seat than it is from the backseat.

Len discovered that, too. I'll bet the fingerprints of his one good hand are still imprinted in the dashboard of that truck.

I managed to slide the truck off into a ditch before we got home. Len was a little wild-eyed, but nobody was hurt; in fact, the kids wanted to do it again. The problem was, we were so far out in the boonies that we had to wait awhile before someone happened by to pull us out.

By the time we got home, it was nearly dark and I still had to feed and water the animals, which was about a two-hour job; the hard-packed ice made it almost impossible to stay on my feet, and in view of Len's unfortunate "ice follies" performance, I needed to be extra careful. One broken bone was about all our household could handle.

It was bitter cold and pitch dark when I finished feeding the animals. As I inched my way down the hill to our trailer house, I was so grateful that it was my last trip for the night. I was numb with cold and kept imagining myself sitting in my kitchen, drinking a steaming cup of chicken noodle soup. Actually, I thought how nice it would be to have a big dishpan of hot chicken noodle soup to soak my feet in.

As I started to open the gate to our yard, I heard a pitiful whine. I turned around and saw our dog Sidney standing on the edge of our cellar hole, looking down at something that was really upsetting him.

Our cellar hole was just that: an eight-by-ten hole that was dug when they put in our water well. We planned to have it made into a cellar in the spring. The place that would eventually be the steps into the cellar was, at this point, just a steep incline of solid ice.

In the bottom of the hole was Sidney's true love, Minnie Mae. Minnie Mae was a big, beautiful German shepherd who belonged to the people down the road. She was crippled in her hind legs, which didn't hamper her running and jumping ability, but at that moment her condition definitely hampered her ability to climb out of that hole. She couldn't get the traction she needed.

Putting my noodle soup fantasy on hold, I got a rope and tied it to the fence post by the cellar hole, and while Len stood in the doorway of the trailer, supervising the rescue mission, I lowered myself down the incline and into the hole. It was great! I felt just like some heroine on one of those Saturday afternoon TV shows. I mean, I had just lowered myself by rope into a dark hole to make a daring rescue! Move over, Wonder Woman!

But after I got down there, I realized that getting into the hole was as far as my plan went. Minnie Mae was happy to see me, but she gave me a look that said, "Okay, now what?"

Lifting her up and out was out of the question . . . we were standing in an eight-foot-hole. Besides, Minnie looked like a sausage with legs. She obviously enjoyed her doggy victuals.

I tried to get behind her and push her up the incline, but I couldn't get enough traction for that. My TV heroine character was beginning to take on cartoon characteristics.

The harder I tried, the more exhausted I became. Finally, I decided I'd go ahead and climb out, warm up a bit, and then call Minnie's family to come and help. I didn't know them, but after all, it was *their* dog.

Much to my surprise, I discovered that I was too pooped to pull myself back up the incline. That would have been all right if I had been a real TV heroine. Then the local TV hero would have been in the wings, waiting to leap into the dark, cold abyss to save me.

As it was, my hero was standing in the wings with his "wing in a sling," shouting instructions to me. Really good ones, too, like, "Pull harder!"

Maybe those instructions did help because with a final surge of determination, I held onto the rope and pulled myself . . . halfway up. Then my feet slid out from under me, and I was left stretched out full-length on the incline, holding onto the rope. But all was not lost. Right before I let go of the rope and slid back down into the hole, Minnie saw her golden opportunity and ran up my back as if it were a ladder. When she got to the top of my head, she planted her front feet firmly in my scalp and with a mighty leap, was out of the cellar hole! After I slid back to the bottom, I looked up to see Minnie and Sidney peering down at me. I could have sworn I heard Minnie say, "Ta-Dummmm!"

So, back to square one . . . Well, not exactly square one. After all, Minnie was out.

I called to Len to send Jim to the toolshed for the hatchet so I could chop some footholds in the ice. But he said that there was an electric cable buried someplace in the vicinity of the incline and I would light myself up like a Christmas tree if I hit it. So much for *that* idea.

Then Len found the answer: "I'll call the neighbors at the end of the road and see if they can come and pull you out with their pick-up truck!"

"No way!" I yelled. "I'll stay in this hole till spring before I'll let somebody I don't even know come down here and pull me out with a truck, like some old cow in a mud bog!"

"Do you know how long it is until spring?" he asked.

"Just lower me down a bucket of chicken noodle soup," I said in the most wistful, frozen martyr's voice I could muster.

Then, as if the thought of hot soup thawed out my brain a bit, I remembered something. Before I picked up Len at the hospital, I had stopped at the feed store and bought a twenty-pound bag of salt to sprinkle on the ground between the barn and our trailer house so I could walk without falling. But Len had said that when the ground thawed out, the salt could work its way down into our water supply. At this point, though, the water supply was the last thing on my mind.

The salt was still in the truck where Len couldn't get to it. Jim was too small to lift it, but Len gave him a bucket and had him go out there and scoop salt out of the bag and into the bucket. Then Jim stood at the top of the cellar hole and threw handfuls of salt all over the incline. I waited a few minutes and then . . . Ta-Dummm!

Jesus said that we are the "salt of the earth." We give a flavor to life that can help make it a little more palatable.

> "Just lower me down a bucket of chicken noodle soup," I said in the most wistful, frozen martyr's voice I could muster.

Maybe, just maybe, we're also salt on a frozen uphill path that someone is trying to climb. I like to think of it like that.

Connie Breedlove

LEARNING TO WALK AGAIN

When I was little, Dibby's cousin had a dog, just a mutt, and the dog was pregnant. I don't know how long dogs are pregnant, but she was due to have her puppies in about a week. She was out in the yard one day and got in the way of the lawn mower, and her two hind legs got cut off. They rushed her to the vet and he said, "I can sew her up, or you can put her to sleep if you want, but the puppies are okay. She'll be able to deliver the puppies."

Dibby's cousin said, "Keep her alive."

So the vet sewed up her backside and over the next week the dog learned to walk. She didn't spend any time worrying, she just learned to walk by taking two steps in the front and flipping up her backside, and then taking two steps and flipping up her backside again. She gave birth to six little puppies, all in perfect health. She nursed them and then weaned them. And when they learned to walk, they all walked like her.

Gilda Radner

KNOCK, KNOCK, WHO'S THERE?

Got a cat door? Is it clearly labeled?

My friend Sue's wasn't, and she walked into her house to find a raccoon in a prized cloisonne bowl, eating Easter candy.

Not only did he forget he was not a cat—he thought he was a bunny!

His brother thought he was a frog. He was playing in the toilet.

Margaret Bigger

You Know You're a Dog Person When . . .

You have a kiddie wading pool in the yard, but no small children.

Lintwheels are on your shopping list every week.

You have baby gates permanently installed at strategic places around the house, but no babies.

The trash can is more or less permanently installed in the kitchen sink, to keep the dog out of it while you're at work.

You can't see out the passenger side of the windshield because there are noseprints all over the inside.

Poop has become a source of conversation for you and your significant other.

Your dog sleeps with you.

You have 32 different names for your dog. Most make no sense, but the dog understands them all.

You like people who like your dog. You despise people who don't.

You carry dog biscuits in your purse or pocket at all times.

You talk about your dog the way other people talk about their kid.

You put an extra blanket on the bed so your dog is more comfortable.

Dog-tracker.com

3

Oink, Chirp, Cackle, and Moo—the Language of Animals

As Dr. Doolittle dreamed, wouldn't it be wonderful if we could just talk to the animals? Alas! We must get along by reading their eyes, their actions, and interpreting the beautiful languages they do speak.

CHICKEN FISHIN'

Our church has a group of older retired men who meet on Tuesday mornings at a local Burger King. I assume they chose BK instead of our own church annex so they could tell lies without the guilt of doing it on the Lord's property. They call themselves the "Romeo Club." Romeo stands for: "Retired Old Men Eating Out." Their weekly sessions have proven to be an endless source of humor and storytelling.

The dean of the bunch is an old mountain man from up around Blue Ridge, Georgia. "Bill" grew up on a small hillside farm in the heart of the north Georgia mountains. He was one of the older among several siblings, and the valedictorian troublemaker of the entire clan. If there was an opportunity for mischief lurking anywhere nearby Bill could sniff it out better than a blue tick on a coon hunt.

One late summer day Bill's mama gave him a chore to ramrod. With fall and winter approaching in the mountains, the chimneys and fireplaces would need to be thoroughly cleaned out. Few things in the hills were more dangerous and threatening to the well-being of the family cabin than a raging creosote fire in an old flue.

Other than being the family heathen, one of Bill's other qualities was his quick, sharp, creative mind. This was, in truth, his only redeeming trait. As far as manual labor was concerned, Bill was "sorry as gully dirt," as his daddy readily admitted to friend and stranger alike. This combination, however, served him well as he continually searched for and usually found ingenious ways of getting out of chores.

Cleaning out chimneys was fieldhand work, Bill reasoned. The wheels in his head began to turn.

From his shady perch on the floor of the back porch he could hear the sound of daddy's eight prize settin' hens as they milled around the back part of the cabin pecking out their afternoon meal. Suddenly, like an epiphany from above, it came to him.

Bill called to his younger brothers and ordered them to run to the corn crib and bring him an ear of the family's scrub corn. He then sent his youngest sister, who was far too innocent to see the plan that was taking shape, to the barn to retrieve a couple of daddy's good cane fishing poles. Bill told them to meet him around front as he trotted off to find the family's homemade ladder. "We're gonna' go chicken fishing," he whispered.

When all the pieces were in place, Bill and his brothers climbed to the top of the cabin with their cane poles. Once there, they baited the hooks with the corn and lowered them down almost to ground level. Bill then told his sister to herd the chickens around toward the area where the baited hooks were waiting.

Bill's sister had great difficulty coercing the chickens to head in the right direction, but finally they showed up and began to peck at the corn on the fish hooks. The original thought was that the chickens would swallow the corn like a fish would have. When they only pecked at the corn, the baited hooks would flitter back and forth in every conceivable direction. Bill and his brothers were having a devil of a time keeping the bait in front of the chickens.

An added dimension involved making just enough noise so that Mama would hear from inside the cabin and think that her boys were complying with her instructions. Too much hoofing around on the roof would surely coax Mama outside to investigate, and thus bring down maternal fire and brimstone once she found out what was up.

Finally deciding that the chickens would not cooperate as he had hoped, Bill enacted plan B. He began "gigging" the chickens in the neck with the fish hooks. Once he had set the hook firmly in the chicken's neck, he and his brothers would pull each of the screaming victims to the roof of the cabin, dislodge the hook, and stuff the bird down into the chimney. His theory was that the flapping of the fowl wings as the chickens descended would dislodge the built-up creosote and thus clean the flue.

Bill's plan did not allow for at least three significant contingencies: One, what to do if the chickens got stuck on the

> Bill's sister had great difficulty coercing the chickens to head in the right direction, but finally they showed up and began to peck at the corn on the fish hooks.

way down. Two, what to do if the creosote was hardened past the point of being affected by the fluttering of the wings. Three, how to explain to Mama what those prize settin' hens were doing coming out of the cabin's fireplaces screaming to the top of their lungs.

The whole experiment turned out to be a miserable failure. The process removed precious little of the creosote, three of the chickens got permanently stuck and had to be put out of their misery before being removed from the chimney, and at least one of the chickens got the better of Bill—pecking him profusely around the neck and ears before flying off. Also, Mama eventually did come outside to investigate the ruckus and received an appreciable shower of chicken fecal matter as the surviving hens flew overhead on their way to safer ground. In the end Bill and his brothers each received their just reward from Daddy's razor strap when he came in from the fields that evening.

The next day Bill was seen back on the roof of the family cabin with his arm stuck down the chimney finally doing the job right. His two brothers were inside attempting to catch the falling creosote in two large tow sacks. His sister, having been given a parental pardon due to her age, continued her daily routine of playing in the creek—her stripes having been partitioned among the three brothers. Mama and Daddy sat longer than normal at the kitchen table at dinner (the term used for "lunch" in the country) discussing Bill's certain future as an inmate in the Georgia correctional system.

And, there wasn't one chicken anywhere to be found.

David Decker

BOILING BIRDS

Did you know that the inscription on the metal bands used by the U.S. Department of the Interior to tag migratory birds, has been changed? The bands used to bear the address of the Washington Biological Survey, abbreviated:

Wash. Biol. Surv.

Until the agency received the following letter from a camper:

> Dear Sirs
>
> While camping last week I shot one of your birds. I think it was a crow. I followed the cooking instructions on the leg tag and I want to tell you, it was horrible.

The bands are now marked Fish and Wildlife Service.

Knight-Ridder News Service

••

I think I live near an animal-testing laboratory. The other day I spotted a mouse wearing hair gel.

Adam Gropman

••

A COOL BIRD

Ben and Jake, two college students, bought a parrot from a pet shop. The parrot was highly intelligent, but all he ever did was swear. He had an amazing vocabulary. He could swear for five minutes straight without repeating himself. At first the two roommates thought it was the coolest bird ever, but after days and nights of constant verbal abuse and obscenities, even the students couldn't take it anymore.

"Dude, we're gonna have to teach that bird a lesson," Ben said.

He grabbed the parrot by the neck and stuck him in the refrigerator. "That'll cool him off a bit!"

For the first few seconds the bird kicked and clawed and thrashed. Then suddenly everything was very quiet.

The two students started to worry that the bird might be hurt, so Jake opened the fridge.

The parrot calmly climbed onto Jake's outstretched arm and said in a very polite manner: "Awfully sorry about the trouble I gave you. I'll do my best to improve my vocabulary from now on."

Ben and Jake were totally amazed. They couldn't understand the transformation that had come over the parrot.

After a few minutes the parrot asked: "By the way, what did that chicken do?"

Oliver Gaspiritz

I WANNA BE A BEAR . . .

If you're a bear, you get to hibernate. You do nothing but sleep for six months. I could deal with that. Before you hibernate, you're supposed to eat yourself stupid. I could deal with that, too.

If you're a bear, you birth your children (who are the size of walnuts) while you're sleeping and wake to partially grown, cute cuddly cubs. I could definitely deal with that.

If you're a mama bear, everyone knows you mean business. You swat anyone who bothers your cubs. If your cubs get out of line, you swat them too. I could deal with that.

If you're a bear, your mate EXPECTS you to wake up growling. He EXPECTS that you will have hairy legs and excess body fat.

Yup . . . I wanna be a bear.

"First my ball rolled under the sofa, then my water dish was too warm, then the squeaker broke on my rubber pork chop. *I've had a horrible day and I'm totally stressed out!!!*"

MY DOG, THE GENIUS

Newsweek magazine recently came out with a cover story entitled "How Smart Are Animals?"

Pretty smart, concluded the reporters, who told of chimps who know sign language, a horse that could count, and pigeons with remarkable memories.

I wasn't surprised to find out animals know as much as they do because I live with Catfish, the black Lab, whose intelligence is often astounding.

Even when he was a puppy, he was bright. When he committed an indiscretion on my living-room rug, I said to him, sternly, "Catfish, never do that on my living-room rug again!"

Sure enough, the next time he didn't go on the living-room rug. He went on the rug in the den. He also learned at a very early age that if he kept whining, no matter how long I ignored him, I finally would give in and share the food on my plate with him. He's especially fond of pizza.

As he got older, Catfish became even smarter. He discovered that twice a week, at approximately 6 A.M., a guy shows up in a truck to take away my garbage.

After that, at the precise moment the garbage truck drove into my driveway, Catfish would come to my bed and bark directly into my ear at a decibel level only slightly lower than a train wreck to awaken me to the fact a stranger was making off with our garbage.

It is only recently Catfish stopped doing that. Once he heard the Supreme Court had ruled a person's garbage is not private, he figured why bother protecting ours any longer.

Catfish's vocabulary also amazes me.

He knows the word "go," for instance. When I say that word, regardless of context, he immediately races to the garage and scratches on my car door. My dog is making Earl Scheib, the famous car painter, a fortune.

Catfish also knows the word "no."

Whenever I say that word, it's a signal to ignore me completely.

Catfish even knows the word "Domino's." He hears that, he knows there's pizza involved, and he drools on my trouser leg.

What Catfish also knows is how to get to me. He does it with those eyes.

How do dogs know they can get anything they want if they just look at you with those sad, loving eyes that ask, "What about me?" and plead, "Please don't go."

Catfish does it to me when I leave him. Those eyes.

"I'll be back in three days," I say.

Those eyes.

"I've got to go. It's business."

Those eyes.

"Okay, you can invite all your friends over for pizza and moon-howling while I'm gone. I'll call Domino's from the airport."

It's tough living with an animal who's smart enough to know a sucker when he sees one.

Lewis Grizzard

EEE-I-EE-I-OUCH!

When my husband Len and I made our big move to the country, we went with visions of a quiet, genteel, country life. Our children would have incredibly rosy cheeks from breathing all that fresh air and eating all those home-grown veggies. There would be fresh bread from the oven, fresh milk from the cow, and fresh eggs from the chickens. What we didn't think about was that all that fresh stuff didn't just happen—it had to be weeded, baked, milked, and gathered.

By the time we got through milking, weeding, baking, and gathering, "genteel" was out the window.

Besides that, there was nothing "genteel" about the roads. We left pieces of our car up and down that road every time we went to town. But that wasn't such a bad thing, because we lived so far out of town that when we first moved out there I kept getting lost. It worked kind of like Hansel and Gretel. I'd go to town and then just follow my car parts home. Sometimes I'd follow the wrong car parts and end up at a strange house, but that was a great way to meet the neighbors.

Well, maybe I'm exaggerating just a little, but one thing I'm not exaggerating is our first winter out there. It was the worst winter that anyone could remember. It sleeted every day for several weeks. The temperature stayed around five or six degrees in the daytime and dipped below zero at night. It was awful!

> By the time we got through milking, weeding, baking, and gathering, "genteel" was out the window.

By that time we had managed to become the proud owners of a calf, two pigs, six rabbits, three dogs, and we probably would have added a partridge in a pear tree to the menagerie if Len had thought about it. I say "Len" because he's the one who wanted all those farm animals. I wanted a dog and two goldfish—and maybe a partridge in a pear tree, but not cows and pigs and all those things old McDonald had, because I'll tell you something else old McDonald had—a tired wife.

At first, Len enjoyed those animals and took care of them—until he slipped on the ice and broke his arm. He had to have surgery on his elbow and was in the hospital for three days.

Now, I am a very sympathetic person, and I felt sorry for him when it happened because I know it really did hurt. But by the time his three-day hitch in the hospital was over, the truth of the situation had begun to sink in, and I really thought about breaking his other arm.

Our son, Jim, was in the second grade and Chris, our daughter, was eighteen months old. The second day that Len was in the hospital, Chris got sick and I had to take her to the doctor, pick Jim up from school, take them to my sister's house in town, and then go back out and feed old McDonald's menagerie, which took me until after dark to finish.

So by the time Len was able to come home, with a cast up to his shoulder and instructions to stay in the house until the sleet and ice melted, I knew that unless those animals learned to brown-bag it, I had a whole new world waiting for me. I also figured out that in that song about Old McDonald, his wife wrote the part that says "ee-i-ee-i-oh"!

The cold weather made taking care of the animals harder than usual because their drinking water would freeze. Since there was no water in the barnyard area, I had to haul water back and forth in a bucket twice a day. If I could have put the same number of miles on a motor home that I put walking back and forth to the barn, carrying water, I could have seen the entire United States and half of Canada—and kept my feet dry while I did it.

The calf was the biggest problem—literally. That calf was six months old and weighed around seven hundred pounds. I'm talking twenty-eight hundred quarter-pounders here. You know that ad where they sing about having your burger your way? Well, maybe at their drive-thru window, but when those burgers are on the hoof, it's a different story.

If I'd had it my way, that calf would have carried its own bucket to my back door and asked for a drink of water. As it was, it did go to the back door, but it didn't take the bucket, and it didn't go to my back door but to my neighbor's.

My neighbor called and told me the calf was in her back-yard. Her husband was at work, and she was under the care of a chiropractor and wondered if I was going to be able to catch it myself.

By then, I had done so many things by myself for the first time, I didn't really think about it. I just got the rope and started out the door.

"You don't know how to rope a calf!" Len exclaimed, not believing what he was seeing.

"So, what's your point?" I asked a bit tersely, hoping he was about to tell me that he had trained that calf to go to the barn if we whistled.

He thought for a minute and then said, rather lamely, "Throw a wide loop."

That wasn't the answer I'd hoped for.

I stood there for a minute, thinking. Len thought I was thinking about how to throw a wide loop over the calf, but I wasn't. I was visualizing him stranded in the middle of the desert with nothing but day-old bread and peanut butter—no jelly.

There were ten acres of brush and gullies between our house and our neighbor's house. I trudged over there and, as I approached her backyard, I saw her standing by her back door, the calf a few yards away eyeballing the situation.

I made a wide loop in the rope and walked slowly toward the calf, wanting to get as close to it as I could. Much to my surprise, it just stood there, looking at me.

I walked right up to it and slipped the rope around its neck as though I did that sort of thing all the time.

The look on my neighbor's face was great! She was as surprised as I was, but I wasn't letting my surprise show. I was so casual about it, I impressed even myself.

I wanted to say something like, "So, what did you expect, Pilgrim?"

But instead I said, "Why are you having to see a chiropractor?"

I didn't get to hear her answer because about that time the calf was hit with a sudden wave of homesickness. It took off at a dead run for our barn, via ten acres of gullies and brush.

I had wrapped the rope around my wrist for a better hold when I had thought I would be "walking" the calf home. Big mistake.

Bouncing along behind that calf, I spent most of the trip on my posterior rather than on my feet.

I called out to the neighbor what I hoped was a nonchalant, "Bye!" but I think the nonchalance was lost in the translation.

And as for finding out why my neighbor had to see the chiropractor, I could find out when I called her to get his name and phone number.

I learned several things that winter—and that particular day I think I learned why John Wayne walked the way he did.

Walking with the Lord soothes a lot of the bruises and scrapes we get from being dragged through life's gullies and brush.

Connie Breedlove

DAISY

The following personals ad appeared in a newspaper:

SBF (Single Black Female) Seeks Male companionship, ethnicity unimportant.

I'm a svelte, good-looking girl who LOVES to play. I love long walks in the woods. Hunting. Camping. Riding in your pickup truck.

Fishing trips. Cozy winter nights spent lying by the fire. Candlelight dinners will have me eating out of your hand. Rub me the right way and watch me respond. I'll be at the front door when you get home from work, wearing only what nature gave me. Kiss me and I'm yours.

Call 555-2121 and ask for Daisy.

The phone number was the Humane Society. Daisy was an eight-week-old black labrador retriever.

CHIPPIE

Chippie the budgie never saw it coming. One second he was peacefully perched in his cage. The next, he was sucked in, washed up and blown over.

The problems began when Chippie's owner decided to clean Chippie's cage with a vacuum cleaner. She removed the attachment from the end of the hose and stuck it in the cage. The phone rang and she turned to pick it up. She'd barely said "Hello" when ssopp! Chippie got sucked in.

The bird owner gasped, put down the phone, turned off the vacuum and opened the bag. There was Chippie—still alive but stunned.

Since the bird was covered in dust she grabbed him and

raced to the bathroom, turned on the tap, and held Chippie under the running water. Then, realizing that Chippie was soaked and shivering, she did what any compassionate bird owner would do—she reached for the hair dryer and blasted the pet with hot air.

Poor Chippie never knew what hit him.

A few days after the trauma, the reporter who'd initially written about the event contacted Chippie's owner to see how the bird was recovering. "Well," she replied, "Chippie doesn't sing much anymore—he just sits and stares."

It's not difficult to see why.

J. John and Mark Stibbe

• •

I like pigs. Dogs look up to us, cats look down on us, but pigs treat us as equals.

Winston Churchill

• •

© Patrick McDonnell. King Features Syndicate.

HELLO, COOKIE

If you ever visit the zoo's Australian section, be sure to stop by the cockatoo exhibit for a while. They are beautiful, entertaining, and some of them even talk. They have often been people's pets before coming to the zoo, and about half of their owners named them Cookie. This is easy to determine because most of the previously owned birds say, "Hello, Cookie."

Mark Gentry enjoyed the ability of being able to impersonate the cockatoos' voices. One could not tell which was the bird and which was Mark. Mark was their keeper. He would often hear patrons attempting to strike up conversations with the cockatoos that talked, and one afternoon he had a bright idea. He stationed himself in the shrubbery next to the exhibit and waited for some enthusiastic visitors to respond to the cockatoos' endless chatter. If a patron repeated one of the bird's phrases, Mark was set up for several minutes of a Candid Camera-type encounter without a camera.

"Hello, Cookie," offered a bird.

"Hello, Cookie," answered a patron.

"What's your name?" entered Mark, but you couldn't tell it was Mark because he sounded just like the cockatoos.

"My name is Barbara," answered a rather attractive patron. Then she would add, "What's yours?"

"Cookie, silly. You just said 'Hello Cookie,' so I thought you knew," said Mark. Barbara still thought she was talking to a bird. She usually caught on when one of the birds said, "So, Barbara, what's your telephone number?"

One day a rather loud, critical, overfed, and unattractive lady brought her little tiny husband to the zoo. Perhaps you might form an accurate mental picture if I simply told you that on that day we could account for the whereabouts of at least one of Cinderella's stepsisters. Her face was adorned with a permanent frown and her demeanor suggested that she was just daring something good to happen so she could step on it.

Her husband just stood there, "Yes, darling"-ed her as she berated the zoo, its animals, the zoo food, and him.

Mark was in the bushes and one of the cockatoos said, "Hello, Cookie."

The lady stared at the bird for a second and responded with, "Hello, Cookie, yourself."

In the twinkling of an eye, Mark responded with, "Hi ya, Fatso."

She gave the closest cockatoo a stare that would have frozen the Medusa, then she clobbered her husband with her purse and said, "Henry, let's get out of here." She stormed off fully convinced that she had been insulted by a bird.

Life truly is a zoo.

Gary Richmond

•••

There is the story of a hen and a pig that left the farm and went into town. Walking down the street, they saw the sign: Ham and Eggs.

The pig said, "Look there; for you that's just a contribution, but for me that's total sacrifice."

Leroy Brownlow

If a pig loses its voice, is it disgruntled?

Author unknown

•••

"I'm only going to live about 12 years. I made
a list of all the things I want to do before I die!"

CANARY CAPER

Once a year, on Valentine's Day, Mama paired the male
and female birds and asked God's blessing on their union.
Come spring, dozens of baby canaries hatched, and we
moved all the families to the aviary my daddy had built in
the garden. Christian picked out a nice shady spot where he
could watch the canaries fly around in the big structure
wrapped in wire netting.

Then one afternoon Mama called urgently: "I forgot to
close the latch on the aviary door! Some of the birds have
escaped!" I rushed outside. "They're only babies," Mama
cried. "They're sure to get lost or hurt!" At that moment
Christian got up from his place in the shade and stretched. Or
eaten, I thought.

We crept slowly to two yellow birds peeking out of a bush.
"Stay there," I whispered as Mama advanced with the net.
She brought it down with a whoosh, but the birds flew right
out from under it in a flash.

"Where'd they go?" she asked.

"There's one!" I called, spotting a shot of yellow in a tree. "And there! And there!" Canaries were everywhere! Mama ran back and forth with her net as Christian fixed his gaze on one hapless creature perched on a low branch. Our cat crouched low to the ground, ready to pounce.

"No!" Mama cried, but Christian sprang through the air and snatched the baby bird in his jaws. I covered my eyes. I couldn't watch. It was too gruesome even to imagine.

"My, oh my!" Mama said. Strangely enough, I heard relief in her voice.

I peeked through my fingers. Mama was just putting the captured bird back in its cage as the cat caught another one! Christian padded over to Mama and ever so gently placed the frightened ball of feathers in her hands. Then he rescued another.

When he had seen all the escaped canaries safely home, Christian lay back down in the shade. I'd say he was smiling— like the cat who didn't eat the canaries.

Myrtle "Cookie" Potter

DUCK, DUCK, GOOSE

When Jan Coleman and her family moved out to the country after life in the city, her two young daughters were excited to live on a farm and couldn't wait to learn how farm life worked.

The first lesson they learned was the facts of life. Among the many animals on the farm were ducks, chickens, and geese. Three pairs of geese, to be exact. As Jan was explaining the birds and the bees to her daughters, she told them that geese mate for life.

Unfortunately, one goose died.

Her girls were heartbroken. "Now what's going to happen, Mom?" they asked. "She's going to be single!"

No problem. The goose took up with a duck.

Then the goose laid a nice big egg. She warmed it and turned it, but nothing happened. She wouldn't budge, she wouldn't leave it, no matter how much the kids coaxed. She was determined to be a mother. Since goose eggs usually hatch in thirty days, after forty-five days, they all began to worry.

Jan's clever girls then had the bright idea to give the goose some eggs from their very prolific banty hen. And twenty-one days later, they hatched.

Mother goose was delighted with her new brood, never noticing that they didn't bear even the slightest resemblance to her, even down to their lack of webbed feet. A short time later, Mama Goose did what comes naturally and headed to the pond for a swim. Her brood devotedly followed Mom into the water.

Only problem is, chickens can't swim.

Splash, splash, sink, sink.

As Mama goose honked frantically and swam in circles around her rapidly shrinking kids, Jan rescued the baby chicks from the water and set them on dry land. Undaunted, one immediately tried to head back to the pond again, so from then on, Jan had no choice but to segregate.

Laura Jensen Walker

••

To err is human; to moo, bovine.

••

Eat, sleep, chew on toy . . . I don't know, Rex, my schedule's getting pretty full. I think I can fit you in right after I bark at the neighbor's cat on Thursday.

SAMMIE AND SUGAR

One day after Kindergarten, Autumn, our five-year-old granddaughter, was home to take her nap—with the dogs as usual. She was sitting on the bed listening to me explain about Sammie, our American Eskimo. He had just been diagnosed with cancer. I explained to Autumn what that meant and that Sammie may have only a few more months to be here with us.

While explaining to her once again that God needed Sammie in heaven, she stopped me to tell me that she was going to pray for God to take Sugar instead. I asked her why and her reply was that Sammie was sweet and Sugar was snappy and not a very nice dog. Plus, Sugar was my dog, and since I was so old I had had a lot of dogs, but she was just five-years-old and it wasn't fair for God to take Sammie as she liked him the best.

I couldn't explain it to her again, except that we needed to pray for Sammie. And pray we did.

Sammie lived five more years and so did Sugar. God hears His children's prayers.

Suzanne Berk

WHY NOT PET EXEMPTIONS?

I'm thinking of writing a letter to the Internal Revenue Service to protest the "Exemptions" section which, at present, limits "dependents" to human beings only. After all, there are plenty of us out here who think income tax returns should be revised to include dependents that are *not* human.

Take dogs, for example. Our small terrier, Mousey, was part of our family for many years. When the can opener whirred, she'd dash to her dog dish where she waited—rolling her marble-like eyes between me and the pet food can. Now I tell you for sure, Mousey was one really *dependent* dog.

Our cat-owner friends claim their "babies" are just as dependent on them as our dog was on us. Other neighbors provide bed and board to two hamsters, a gerbil, three goldfish, and a turtle.

In addition to the above assortment, there's another group of non-human dependents which are in our back yard: chipmunks. They winter in logs behind our house. From spring on, they depend on me to pour sunflower seeds into a certain crack in their log home and to keep an old pie tin filled with fresh water.

Along with the chipmunks are birds which expect bed-and-breakfast service, too. And ready-made birdhouses. Suet balls. And birdbaths close to trees to screen themselves from wandering cats.

Some of those birds are protected species, and if you kill one, you'll be fined and spend time in jail regretting it. Yet do any of us get compensation from our government for all these non-human dependents we feed and shelter and drain dollars from us? No!

And another thing: The IRS allows me deductions on my depreciating, non-human machinery. But what about me? I'm depreciating, too. Fast. But am I allowed depreciation on myself? No. Doesn't make much sense, does it?

Isabel Wolseley Torrey

4

I Don't Wanna Iguana!

Exotic pets are loved by some and abhorred
by others. Frankly, I never met a lizard I liked,
but then they probably don't like me either.
But I love their funny, slimy stories.

THIS LITTLE PIGGY WENT TO DAY CARE

One year my sister Malvina and I merged our energies and opened a day-care business at her house. It was very successful—we had several kids, and we really worked to make it go.

We had craft classes for them, hot lunches, and kindergarten pick-up and delivery. All in all, it was a working mom's dream, if I say so myself. It was also our dream, because having a successful, home-based business was something we had both always wanted.

But the dream soon took on nightmare characteristics, and not just your run-of-the-mill type nightmares. I'm talking Freddy Krueger, here.

It started with our decision to sell homemade candy. Now, I'll be the first to admit that the candy business probably wouldn't have caused a problem by itself; the pig was the big problem—even though it was a small pig. But I'm getting ahead of myself.

It was Christmas time, and we had this great family recipe for a date nut candy log that we decided to try to sell for extra Christmas money.

In the afternoons, when the kids were having their naps, my sister would take candy samples to give out in the stores and get orders for the candy. I would stay with the kids and make candy to fill the orders we already had. It was working out great.

Then one afternoon Malvina was out getting orders, the kids were napping, and I was up to my ears in date nut candy when the phone rang. When I answered it, my husband's voice said, in an overly cheerful tone, "Hi! What are you doing?"

I couldn't understand why he was asking me that; he knew what I was doing.

"Well," I said, flicking a crumb of candy off my shoulder, "for the last hour I've been soaking in a warm bubble bath, and now I'm sitting here waiting for the maid to finish fixing my lunch."

He laughed and made small talk for a few minutes until finally, he said, "Well, I've got to get back to work. Oh, by the way, I got a pig today."

"By the way, you got a pig today?" I repeated.

"Yeah, I was going to surprise you, but I couldn't wait. So, what do you think?"

"Flowers would have been nice," I said.

"Honey, this was such a good deal, I couldn't pass it up," he said.

"But it's Christmas time; how can we afford a pig?"

"That's the best part! It was free!"

"Free?" I said, almost afraid to ask the rest of the question.

"Why would anyone give away a pig? And even if it was free, we don't have a pig house or a fence or anything."

"It's not called a pig house, it's called a pigsty," he said, his voice dripping with patience.

"Why was it free and where are we keeping it?" I said, my voice totally devoid of patience.

"Let me explain before you get upset. This is a very small pig . . ."

"So, where are we going to keep a very small pig?" I asked.

There was a long enough pause to cause my apprehension level to hit TILT.

"We'll have to keep it in the house for a while," he finally managed to say.

Now, keep in mind, this happened several years before people started keeping miniature pigs as pets. This happened when a pig was a pig and by any other name was still a pig.

"No!"

"Honey, it's so tiny! It's in a shoe box!"

"No, no, no, NO!"

"It's mother rejected it," he said.

"I don't blame her," I answered.

"We'll talk about it this evening. I've got to get back to work. Bye," he said, and I was left listening to the dial tone.

The first thing Len did when we got home that night was to take the pig out of the box and give it to me to hold. This man was a real pro. He knew exactly what he was doing. That pig really *was* so tiny that it was in a shoe box, and it *was* really cute. There I was, holding that sweet, little pig while I told Len how impossible it would be to take care of one so small.

He reached over and took the pig from me, saying, "You're right. I don't know what I was thinking. This pig would require way too much care, and neither one of us has that much time."

"What are you going to do with it?" I asked, hoping he would say he knew of a home for pigs.

"It'll have to be destroyed," he said, putting on his jacket.

"No!" I yelled, snatching the pig from him with all the ferocity of an enraged mama pig who was protecting her own.

"But, honey, there's no way you'll have time to do this."

"Yes, I will, I will."

"Okay, if you're sure," he said, taking an eyedropper out of his coat pocket. "You can feed it with this. I'll set the alarm to go off every two hours so it won't miss a feeding. Goodnight, little mama."

As I watched him disappear down the hall and into our bedroom, my motherly instincts suddenly began to wane. He will never know how close he came to getting hit in the back of the head with a flying pig.

The next morning I got up with circles under my eyes from three nighttime feedings. I felt guilty because the last time I fed the pig, I found myself mentally measuring it for a hoagie bun.

After I had a couple of cups of coffee to get my nerve geared up, I called my sister to try and explain why I was going to have to bring a pig with me that morning.

"I think this is going to be one of those days," she said, laughing. "I thought you just said you were bringing a pig with you."

"I did say that," I said.

"What do you mean, 'a pig'?" she asked, still not realizing I meant a PIG.

"It's a baby pig, and I have to bring it with me because it has to be fed every two hours."

"No!"

"It's a very small pig," I said.

"No! No! No!"

"Its mother rejected it."

Talk about role reversal! I was playing Len, my sister was playing me, and the pig was playing an innocent bystander.

"Look," she said, "even if it is a small pig we can't keep it here because if the parents find out we're keeping a pig in the house, they'll take their kids out of day care. And when word gets around, our candy sales are history."

I hadn't thought of that.

"I just don't know what to do about it," I said.

She thought for a minute and then she said, "Okay, bring it with you, and when you get here, honk the horn. I'll get the kids busy in the other end of the house while you sneak the pig down into the basement."

That plan came off without a hitch. It worked perfectly! It was such a success that after the pig was safely hidden in the basement, I had a tremendous feeling of exhilaration, as if we had just pulled off the hoax of the century. You'd have thought we were dealing with the CIA instead of a group of five-year-olds.

> It was such a success that after the pig was safely hidden in the basement, I had a tremendous feeling of exhilaration, as if we had just pulled off the hoax of the century.

Well, we set the timer on the oven to go off every two hours, and when it buzzed, Malvina would get the kids' attention so I could run down to the basement and feed the pig. This was pretty exhausting, but it worked.

But by that afternoon, my sister was beginning to run out of things with which to distract the kids, and they were beginning to look at her as if maybe she was ready for the Big Day Care Center in the sky.

In between feedings we were catching up on our candy orders. The recipe was incredibly hard to mix since it had chopped dates, marshmallows, pecans, and graham cracker crumbs—it was like trying to mix cold tar.

That afternoon we managed to mix, roll, and wrap thirty-two of those candy logs. We felt as if we had been pulled through a knothole backward, but we also had a tremendous feeling of accomplishment.

Until . . .

While we were standing there admiring our thirty-two date nut rolls stacked like cordwood on the cabinet, I discovered a button missing from my cuff—a button that hadn't been missing when I started mixing the candy.

We searched every nook and cranny in the house, from kitchen to basement. That was the most intense game of "button, button, who's got the button?" that either one of us had ever played.

But it was to no avail. Finally, we both stood mutely staring at the only place we hadn't searched, the thirty-two candy rolls, stacked like cordwood on the cabinet.

"Do you think it's in one of those?" my sister asked in a very tired, lackluster voice.

"Maybe," I said with about one degree less enthusiasm than she was registering.

"So, what now?" I asked.

She just stood there shaking her head for the longest time. I was beginning to think she had developed some sort of nervous tic. Maybe the weight of that missing button was the proverbial "straw that broke the camel's back."

Then she began laughing, quietly at first, like it was some private joke only she knew about. Then the laughter got louder and louder, and the tears began to run down her face and she was gasping for breath.

"What?" I asked, laughing just because she was.

But she couldn't answer. She wasn't even making a sound now. Her mouth was open, and she was obviously laughing, but with a temporary loss of sound.

The harder she laughed, the harder I laughed, until we were both sitting on the floor, almost helpless with laughter.

Finally she said, as she tried desperately to catch her breath, "I know what to do about the candy."

I was laughing too hard to even ask what she had in mind.

But that was all right, she didn't need a straight line, she was on a roll.

"When we deliver the candy, we'll tell them that we hid a button in one of the candy rolls and the person who gets the candy with the button wins a pig!"

That was too much. Everything became a blur of pigs, buttons, candy, and kids, and we laughed and laughed and laughed. After that we felt soooooo much better!

We decided to go ahead and take a chance on delivering the candy, and that was good because a couple of days later we found the button in the silverware drawer.

Unfortunately, the little pig was too young and it didn't make it, but if it had survived, I don't know what we would have done with it. It would definitely have been a pet. We'd have ended up sharing our television and snacks every evening with a three-hundred-pound couch potato.

Connie Macsas Breedlove

CHICKEN

A chicken goes into the library, walks up to the librarian, and says, "Book."

The librarian says, "You want a book?"

"Book."

"Any book?"

"Book."

So the librarian gives the chicken a novel and off it goes. An hour later the chicken comes back and says, "Book-book."

The librarian says, "Now you want two books?"

"Book-book."

So she gives the chicken two more novels. The chicken leaves but again comes back later.

"Book-book-book."

"Three books?"

"Book-book-book."

So the librarian gives the chicken three books, but she decides she'll follow the chicken and find out what's going on. And the chicken goes down the alley, out of town and toward the woods, into the woods and down to the river, down to the swamp, and there is a bullfrog. The chicken sets the books down by him. The bullfrog looks at the books and said, "Reddit . . . Reddit . . . Reddit. . ."

Prairie Home Companion

. . . .

A couple of rabbits were being chased by a pack of coyotes. They stopped in a haystack, and one rabbit said to the other, "We gonna make a run for it, or stay here and outnumber them?"

Red Skelton

. . . .

ATTACK OF THE BUTTERFLY

It soared past me like a bat from hell. "What is that?" I thought. I had just finished pumping gas and was climbing back into my car. Before I could close the door, the monstrous butterfly flew in behind me and executed a ten-point landing on the armrest between seats.

"That's the biggest butterfly I've ever seen," I thought. No way am I closing the door with that thing in my car . . ."shoo!"

The butterfly was oblivious to me. "Look, I don't take hitchhikers!" I spewed. It didn't leave.

I climbed out, leaving the car door open. Maybe it simply

needed a bit of gentle encouragement to direct it to the door. I couldn't bring myself to touch it. Of course, I couldn't find a thing in the car to swat it with except an old church bulletin. I attempted to nudge it toward the open door, but it only moved to a spot further away from me where I couldn't reach it.

"I'll open the hatchback and maybe it will fly out. Get out!" It bared its fangs at me. Okay, maybe it was antenna, but it sure looked like fangs.

I went to the other door and opened it, the better to swat at the bug. I couldn't do it. I didn't want to kill it, just to get rid of it. The church bulletin was a pretty flimsy weapon, but I nudged it again. Apparently, it was not impressed by the schedule of upcoming church events, because it still refused to leave.

"This is getting ridiculous!" It must like sports cars. Why else would anyone prefer to drive instead of flying? I briefly considered throwing it the car keys, and saying, "Take it, the tank is full." No one will ever believe I was carjacked by a bug with a fear of flying.

I was beginning to get that helpless female feeling that I hate, but tried to devise a plan. Tear gas? Mace? 911? I don't think so. About that time a knight in shining armor came out of the gas station. Okay, it was only a guy in a T-shirt and jeans who had paid for his gas and was headed for his pickup truck. Who says knights have to wear armor these days?

I appealed to his macho side. "Are you afraid of bugs?" I yelled around the gas pump.

He looked at me crumbly, and shook his head "no." Big mistake.

"Would you mind getting this bug out of my car?" I asked, not mentioning that a moth the size of Count Dracula was lurking behind the passenger seat.

He came over to investigate, armor clinking. Apparently the moth, butterfly, or whatever it was, sensed I was bringing in reinforcements and decided to retreat. With a swish and flutter of wings, it suddenly took flight and shot out the door right past Lancelot's face. He ducked and we watched in wonder as the moth did a hammerhead and several double loops before it streaked away into the wild blue yonder. I half expected it to leave a trail of smoke behind.

"Well, guess you don't have to do anything after all" I said. He seemed relieved to be excused from duty.

I quickly slammed my car doors and sped away, keeping an eye on the rearview mirror for a butterfly with fangs coming up behind me at 80 mph. So far that is the last I've seen of the thing, though.

The butterfly is probably back at the cocoon right now telling his mate what a bad day he had, and how he is late getting home from work because he accidentally flew into the car of a crazy lady who assaulted him with a church bulletin.

Sheila Moss

••

A woman opened her Westinghouse refrigerator to find a live white rabbit seated on the top shelf.

"What in the world are you doing here?" the surprised woman asked.

"Well," the rabbit replied, "this is a Westinghouse, and I'm just westing."

Rusty Wright and Linda Raney Wright

••

COWS

Apparently I'm not the only one bitten with the idea of living something of a cowgirl—or cowboy's—life. I have some good friends who, soon after their son went off to Duke, got cows. They can't say why, and they can't say why, either, they have named them after opera singers.

Maybe it's the size of the cows' chests, or the way they can stand in the back of the pasture and bellow as though their long lost love has gone off to McDonald's. But according to my friends, there is something in the general nature of the animal that wants to sing.

The first one they got was a black bull they named Carlo Bergonzi. Pretty soon they had a herd of eight cows who each night would meet my friends at the front gate as they drove home from work. Cows don't have much expression in general, but after a couple of months my friends said their cows developed definite moods that they felt compelled to read. In the evening, as soon as my friends pulled into their driveway, their cows would hang their heads over the fence and walk ever so slowly to escort the car into the garage. Along the way, my friends could look over each cow and talk about whether or not he or she was putting on weight, seemed to be happy, depressed, or looked antsy.

Apparently it's important to have a contented cow. If a cow is supposed to become meat or give milk, it's best that the cow stay oblivious to all this and go on thinking he's out in green pastures forever and for no reason. These cows that my friends have are of the meat variety, bred to become T-bones, stew, and to appear in spaghetti. But when my friends' cows took on the names of Bergonzi and Pavarotti and Marilyn and Beverly, my friends became vegetarians. Now they are quick to give you their twenty-five recipes for beans.

Apparently it's important to have a contented cow.

Over the months, the cow herd has expanded and so has their relationship with my friends. Each night now the cows not only meet my friends and escort them to the garage, they also walk the fence line outside of the house, following my friends as they go from room to room. The herd begins at the kitchen, then moves on to the windows of the family room, then finally to the bedroom, until the last light is turned out.

The only problem my friends now have is that their cow herd is getting so big they recently had to give their backyard over to pasture. One night my friends were awakened by a baritone, or at least that's what they said. It was an impassioned singing followed by a loud crash like cymbals being used somewhere out in the pasture. When they turned on the back porch lights, they saw Bergonzi running at a charcoal grill. They had forgotten they had abandoned it in a corner of the patio that they had recently turned into pasture.

Bergonzi was running up under it, putting it over his horns and flipping it high into the air where it would do a somersault, then crash down. No doubt he was doing it for all the cows in the world.

But I didn't ask my friends what he was singing. I didn't need to. I'm pretty sure it was some kind of ode to joy. I'm also pretty sure that next week, when my friends drive up to see their son at Duke, they're going to ask me to baby-sit their cows.

Shelley F. Mickle

FRANK & ERNEST ® by Bob Thaves

IF YOU DON'T MIND THROWING TENNIS BALLS FOR ETERNITY, I DO HAVE AN OPENING IN DOGGIE HEAVEN.

Animal Curiosities

If the plural of "goose" is "geese," is the plural of "moose" "meese"?

What do chickens think we taste like?

What do you call a male ladybug?

When dog food has a new and improved taste, who tests it?

Why didn't Noah swat those two mosquitoes when he had the chance?

God knew a turtle would be too slow to get home for dinner, so He just put him in a mobile home.

If man evolved from monkeys and apes, why do we still have monkeys and apes?

Compiled by Mary Hollingsworth

"The bidding will start at eleven million dollars."

A DOG NAMED COOL-WHIP

All right," his mother relented. "You can keep a puppy. But just one."

A litter of seven small puppies nuzzled next to their mother, Duchess, a registered gold-and-white collie. Duchess had been bred so that the family would benefit from the extra money the puppies would bring. Eleven-year-old Ryan protested as soon as he saw the newborn creatures.

"You can't sell them! You just can't," he protested.

Even though they would go to good homes, it would indeed be hard to let each puppy go. Ryan was close to tears and his mother's heart softened. Finally, she agreed to let him keep one of the puppies as his very own. Kneeling next to Duchess, he cupped one of the small animals in his hands. Duchess allowed him to hold each one until he decided which he would keep.

"This is the one," he told his mother while holding a fine male with the beautiful coloring of his mother. His mother agreed that this puppy would not be sold and would belong to Ryan.

"What about a name?" she asked.

Without hesitation, Ryan replied, "Cool-Whip. I am going to call him Cool-Whip!"

A smile on her lips, his mother had to ask the obvious question: "Why would you name a dog Cool-Whip?"

"Because," Ryan answered calmly, "I've always wanted a dog that had his name on his bowl!"

Cathy Lee Phillips

CAMELS

A mother and baby camel are talking one day when the baby camel asks, "Mom, why have I got these huge three-toed feet?"

The mother replies, "Well son, when we trek across the desert your toes will help you to stay on top of the soft sand."

"OK," said the son. A few minutes later the son asks, "Mom, why have I got these great long eyelashes?"

"They are there to keep the sand out of your eyes on the trips through the desert."

"Thanks, Mom," replied the son. After a short while, the son returns and asks, "Mom, why have I got these great big humps on my back?"

The mother, now a little impatient with the boy, replies, "They are there to help us store fat for our long treks across the desert, so we can go without water for long periods."

"That's great, Mom, so we have huge feet to stop us sinking, and long eyelashes to keep the sand from our eyes, and these humps to store water, but Mom . . ."

"Yes, son?"

"Why the heck are we in the San Diego Zoo?"

Author Unknown

••

Have you ever wondered why, whichever side of the door your pet finds himself, he wants to be on the other?

Mary Hollingsworth

••

FRISKY

During the very early days of El Al [the Israeli airline], their station manager at Heathrow airport occasionally found time to perform extra duties, such as taking any dog for a short walk on the runway while the plane was refueling.

One day, while checking the cargo of a plane that arrived ahead of schedule, the manager noticed a large dog resembling a rather shaggy Alsatian. The dog looked at him with pleading eyes, so the kindly station manager tied a short rope to the dog's neck and led him out onto the runway. The dog happily made exploratory runs, bounding and sniffing about in sheer glee, with the station manager hard put to keep up with the unusually frisky animal.

After some farewell pats the dog was put in his cage, and the manager went back to his office to check his mail. There on his desk was an urgent telegram. It read, "Please be advised that a wolf bound for the London Zoo is on board the plane. Handle with extreme caution!"

Walt and Ann Bohrer

CREEPY CRAWLERS

*H*arald called me yesterday with a story that will send any arachniphobics among my readership into therapy.

Harald is my brother-in-law. He and my sister Renee live in Oak Harbor, Washington, with their three boys, six goldfish, and a tarantula.

The tarantula is a new addition. One week ago, their family roster did not include a spider the size of carry-on luggage.

It all started when my sister Renee decided to go away for the weekend. She was going to a women's retreat. As she was heading out the door, her husband announced that he would be taking the boys to the pet store because seven-year-old Hunter wanted to buy a pet. Harald added, "He wants a tarantula."

"Absolutely no tarantulas," Renee said. "If a spider like that ever got loose in the house, I'd have to move into a hotel. No Best Western, either, I'm talking Hilton."

The next day Harald and the boys were driving in the van, Hunter cradling a glass terrarium on his lap, when Harald said, "Oh yeah. Don't let it get loose in the house or Mom'll have to move to a motel or something."

They arrived home and carried their furry friend into the house. Less than an hour later, one of the boys was holding the terrarium when it fell to the floor and broke into tiny pieces. Harald spied the eight-legged wonder sitting dazed among the glass. He rushed to pick it up. The spider promptly bit Harald's finger. Harald flung the spider to the ground, where it scurried under a kitchen cabinet.

Harald looked at the clock.

Renee was due home in two hours.

Armed with a flashlight and broomstick, Harald probed the small hole into which the black spider had fled. No luck.

Returning from the garage, Harald plugged in a 6.5 horsepower Shop-Vac capable of suctioning the dimples off Joe Namath. But it couldn't dislodge an arachnid from a cabinet.

Undaunted, Harald headed back to the garage. When he returned a few minutes later, he was brandishing an electric saw.

By now several neighborhood husbands had learned of the crisis and gathered 'round to offer hearty masculine support as, piece by piece, Harald began sawing apart his cabinets. The cabinet floor beneath the sink went first. Then various toeplates. Then bottoms of drawers.

They finally found the tarantula in the last possible section of cabinet.

The furry interloper was safely imprisoned in a borrowed terrarium when Renee walked in the front door.

She immediately said, "What happened here?"

Harald said, "Why do you ask?"

"There's a 75-pound Shop-Vac sitting on the white carpet in the middle of the living room, that's why. What's going on?"

The men in my sister's life—all four of them, from the midlifer down to the preschooler—looked her in the eye and said, "Nothing. Nothing happened. Everything's fine."

Around the corner in the kitchen, the cabinets lay in pieces, and sawdust was still settling around the flashlights, saws, and Shop-Vac attachments.

I imagine Renee was about to figure it out on her own.

She didn't have to. Hunter confessed. Then, to make up for all the commotion his pet had caused, he decided to do something extra special for his mom.

He named the spider in her honor. He named it "Mama."

We can learn a lot from this story. We can learn to avoid women's retreats, staying home instead to protect our homestead from well-meaning husbands and venomous spiders larger than most of our body parts.

Renee says that, besides the women's retreat thing, the experience is also teaching her to face her fears. She says, "I don't want to steal Hunter's joy over this pet. So I'm working on putting aside my fears. I make a conscious effort to go look at the tarantula at least once an hour, sometimes twice, just to desensitize myself. Not to mention to make sure he's still in his cage."

> I make a conscious effort to go look at the tarantula at least once an hour, sometimes twice, just to desensitize myself.

Sort of like living with Hannibal Lecter.

Life's like that isn't it? Sometimes our worst fears come home to roost. Sometimes someone leaves, or someone dies, or the stock market crashes, or the doctor clears his throat ominously before delivering the news, and we think, like Job in the Old Testament, "Here it is. This is it. The thing I have feared has come upon me."

And then we get on with the business of coping, which includes, but isn't limited to, activities like crying and whining, which eventually, if we're lucky, begin to morph into other things, things like accepting and trusting and growing.

I wish you and I could be protected from everything that goes bump in the night. Instead, we have a God who says, "Yes, they'll go bump, but let me hold the flashlight, and we'll face it together."

And who knows? When it's all said and done, maybe we'll come out ahead, in possession of things we couldn't have gotten any other way, things like mettle and strength and spirit. Not to mention an eight-inch-long spider named "Mama."

Karen Scalf Linamen

DEAD OR ALIVE?

When asked to look after their house and pets by neighbors who were going away on holiday, the Joneses readily agreed. They duly looked after the dog, but they completely forgot about feeding the rabbit until one day the dog brought it in, dead, muddy, and bloody.

Full of remorse, the Joneses cleaned up the rabbit and put it in the cage, so that it would appear to have died a natural death.

When the neighbors returned, the Joneses received a rather puzzled telephone call from them. They said the rabbit had died the day before they left for their holiday, "and we buried him in the garden."

Nigel Rees

FUR PEOPLE

I've volunteered with an animal rescue group for over ten years. There are some people who think I'm crazy to submit my home and personal life to the ravages that come from having animals in and out on a regular basis. But there are several things I've learned through the years that I wouldn't exchange for any amount of money, new home, or even better furniture.

- If you show a little kindness toward an animal, you will be rewarded sevenfold with love and loyalty in return.
- No matter how much money you make, what kind of clothes you wear, what type of house you own, or what kind of car you drive, you are still the most wonderful person on the planet if you spare a kind word and a pat on the head.

- A warm blanket on a cold night can make the sadness in a pair of eyes disappear.
- Saving a dog from an uncertain future is great, but finding a forever home for that same dog is even better.
- A dog is a great barometer at telling who is friend and who is foe.

If I had the chance to have the yards of carpet back that were ruined by puppy accidents and seniors who just couldn't make it out the door in time; if I had the chance to have my furniture restored with all teeth marks and scratches gone; if I had the chance to have the grass and flower gardens in my backyard in immaculate order, untouched and undisturbed; if I had the chance to have my heart and memories unmarred by tears and scars due to those who didn't make it because of sickness or injuries, would I? No, I wouldn't. My life has been made full because of having all the hundreds of four legged "fur people" come into my home and my heart.

Rhonda Hogan

Cat got your tongue, it's a dog-eat-dog world, cat fur to make kitten britches, it's raining cats and dogs . . . what kind of sick species are you that you people keep coming up with this stuff?

© 2006 Ron Wheeler. www.cartoonworks.com

FERRETS FOR THE FUN OF IT

All my life I've had some kind of animal companion—sometimes my only companionship. I'd like to share with you my memories of two ferrets—Misty and Charlotte. I was strolling downtown in Rutland, Vermont, when a man came along walking two Chows. I had not owned a pet for years; the desire to have one had been tugging away at me. The man let me stroke the thick, soft fur of the two big dogs. Then a woman passed by walking a snake on a leash. An unusual pet, but at least she had one. I stopped in front of Royal Pets . . . then marched in.

My son, Dennis, wanted a dog; I was a cat person. But we rented from someone who wouldn't let us keep either one. I would have to find an animal that stayed in a cage, or at least had one, to pacify the landlord. It was painful to pass the yelping puppies with bright, please-take-me-home eyes, and several fluffy kittens. Amid cages of gerbils, mice, and hamsters, I saw one labeled ferrets.

There were seven of them: wrestling, sleeping, and running through a plastic tube. They were about the size of my hand, with long, furry bodies like weasels, pointed faces, dark, sparkling eyes, and ratlike tails, only with hair. Their energy and playfulness was what really drew me. I went to the desk and told the salesman I wanted to hold one. He handed me a fur piece with dark brown around the front, legs, and hindquarters, brown hairs sprinkled over white fur, and a mask like a raccoon. As soon as I took the soft, wriggling thing—it bit me.

I said, "Put this rodent back in its cage!" I had held many animals, but none of them sunk their teeth into me at first contact.

The man took the ferret and gently flicked his finger under its chin. "That's all you have to do to train her not to bite. They're only six weeks old, that's how they play with each other. Ferrets have tough skin, this little gal didn't think she was hurting you."

Hesitantly, I took the ferret back. Holding her close, I liked the way she felt. The softness of her fur, the way her whiskers tickled, and the tiny pink nose that was poking between my fingers. One ferret really stood out, another female with a white coat and pink eyes. It would be cruel to have just one pet. My son was at school all day and then hung out with his friends, and I worked from eight until four, so one ferret would be alone a lot.

The cage and ferrets were on sale that day. I got the masked bandit and the albino for a bargain price of $100 (ordinarily, that's what one ferret would cost), and $50 for the cage. The pet store attendant told me they'd all been spayed and neutered. He also told me their anal glands had been removed. If not for that operation, I would soon think I lived in a stink bomb factory.

They needed a box and litter, dry cat food (ferrets would eat cat food, rabbit food, or ferret food, cat food being the cheapest), a water bottle, food dish, all the ferret toys I could afford, and a bottle of Linatone, a liquid treat ferrets loved. I also, and wisely I think, bought a ferret handbook. I had to go home and get my car; the cage was too big for me to carry. Three feet by two feet, by two feet (ferrets needed space!).

I moved the new tenants into our one-room apartment. Then I sat in front of the cage and watched the curious little fuzzies explore their new home. They rolled balls around and tried to climb up the sides of the cage. One jumped on the other and they wrestled. Ferociously, I thought, for such small animals.

I had wondered over the years how much affection animals felt for each other. Now I wondered where the mother ferret was and if she missed her brood, and did my ferrets miss the rest of the litter?

Would Dennis and I become their family now? My son was

the only one in our family who lived with me. My daughter, her husband, and my ex-husband lived in Las Vegas, Nevada. Our family was broken up, like the ferret family. Just then Dennis came in. When he saw the ferrets, the first thing he asked was "Who are we keeping them for?" He broke into a big grin when I told him these lively, little critters belonged to us.

I said, "You name them!" He came up with two names surprisingly fast: Misty and Charlotte. Misty was a natural name for an animal with white fur, but I asked, "Who is Charlotte?" He never told me. Dennis poked his fingers in the cage and got bitten before I could explain ferret ways to him.

I said, "Don't touch them until I read the manual." Good thing I checked the handbook before letting the lithe, little things out of their cage. Ferrets could fit through any space that was no smaller than a square inch, and that was a full-grown ferret; these two were babies. Exploring was a ferret's middle name; they would get into anything and everything. The book suggested we hold them for a few days before letting them loose. Misty and Charlotte needed to get to know us as much as we needed to learn about them. The way they were scampering around their cage, making them stay in our laps was going to be a job.

Six months later, Misty and Charlotte fit into our lives like pieces of Velcro coming together—as if there had been a space they were supposed to fill. It was fascinating to watch them scuttling around the apartment in the strange way they moved; their backs formed a hump, then straightened out again, like two fuzzy slinkys.

Dennis liked to show off our furballs to his friends. The guys would be lounging on the bed watching TV when Misty and Charlotte would poke their faces into Levi pockets and drag out wallets. Dennis's friends laughingly accused him of teaching the ferrets to pick pockets.

Charlotte even had a trick she would do with very little

prompting. Dennis or I would set her on the floor underneath a bureau. She would squeeze herself in behind the bureau drawers and climb up. Then she could be heard shuffling around papers and miscellaneous in the top drawer. We would open it and her furry little face and bright eyes would be looking up at us; the closest thing to a magic trick I've ever seen an animal do.

Misty wasn't much for tricks. She was the bigger, stronger ferret and usually won their wrestling matches. Charlotte would jump on her and it would look as if Charlotte had the upper hand, then Misty would roll over and easily take her down, grabbing Charlotte by the scruff of the neck. Dennis and his friends would make small bets on who would win the ferret matches. Misty and Charlotte would wrestle whenever someone came over, as if they were doing it solely to entertain.

The ferret book said the fuzzies would make a noise that sounded like "dook." It was a sound of well-being, like a cat purring. The only sound I ever heard Misty and Charlotte make sounded more like a chicken clucking, but I guess "dook" was close enough. They made that sound often, they must have been content with their lives.

Dennis and his friends would make small bets on who would win the ferret matches.

I remember more quiet times, when the little dookers and I were alone. On one such evening I stroked Misty's long neck and back for a while, then let her slide off my lap, down the sofa, and make her hump-backed way across the room and under the bed. I picked Charlotte up and stroked her for a few minutes. I had given them baths in the sink that morning with ferret shampoo and brushed them. Their fur was soft and glistening. Charlotte got down and went under the bed to find Misty. I watched her go and thought of the first part of a poem by Cecil Frances Alexander:

All things bright and beautiful,
All creatures, great and small,
All things wise and wonderful,
The Lord God made them all.

Things had not been going well on my job; I had been tense and irritable. I heard Misty and Charlotte scrambling around under the bed, then I saw Misty's head and Charlotte's butt as they bit and wrestled. I leaned back on the sofa and relaxed, my problems at work didn't seem so bad or important now.

Misty and Charlotte had been with us for a year when my daughter's baby was born. I decided Dennis and I were moving to Las Vegas. It was time for our family to be together, especially since it had a new member. But that would mean losing two members. Lila had gotten rid of a cat because she was afraid to have it around her baby. I knew my daughter and son-in-law wouldn't want us to show up with two animals that looked like weasels, could wedge themselves into every tiny space in their home, and had sharp teeth.

Besides that, I imagined all kinds of terrible things happening to Misty and Charlotte if they got out in an apartment complex with cats and dogs. And winos and panhandlers— they might end up as some drunk's meal. Our cuddly, furry friends had to go.

Telling myself they were just animals did not make giving them away any easier. I believe pets and their masters form a bond—become family. This would be the second time Misty and Charlotte were torn away from their family. We gave them to one of Dennis's friends. After we were settled in Las Vegas, we called him to ask how our ferrets were doing. He told us, to our surprise and disappointment—he had given them away and their new owner had disappeared.

Over the years I've thought of the cute little twerps. They had the energy of battery-run toys, but were able to sleep like the dead when they needed rest. Watching them snooze peacefully, I began giving my body the rest it needed, and still do. The furry duo was not afraid to explore anything. I explore new ideas and experiences more confidently. When you have pets, there are times you do things just for fun, no other reason. Maybe those frolicking ferrets taught me about life, and I didn't realize it until now.

Jo-Ann Burke Fillion

5

Here, Kitty, Kitty

Is there anything funnier than a batch of kittens that go skittering across the room, rolling, climbing, and doing somersaults? They're hilarious and such wonderful free entertainment.

A CAT NAMED "FIREWOOD"

Sam Stinson wanted only two things for his fourth birthday—he wanted to go camping and he wanted a kitten.

The camping trip was easy enough. Brian and Lynn, Sam's parents, enjoyed camping. They even had a favorite spot at a lake not far from their home. All camping supplies were packed neatly in the garage and it would take only a matter of minutes to load them onto the back of Brian's big purple truck. Lynn purchased food and supplies for the campout, including an appropriate birthday cake for a four-year-old little boy. All things ready, the family set off for Sam's camping celebration at the lake.

But, the cat.

That required a little more deliberation. While Brian and Lynn wanted to teach Sam the responsibility of owning a pet, they wondered whether Sam would soon lose interest in a four-legged fur ball and leave it for them to raise. But, it was hard to deny Sam's request. You see, Sam is their only child and, after all, it wasn't as if he had asked for a horse or anything extravagant. They had no other pets. Also (and I think this was the clincher!), Sam is as cute as they come! It would be awfully hard to say no to that child. With his father's big brown eyes and his mother's blonde hair, Sam is one precious four-year-old. I can only imagine the girls that will be circling the Stinson home when Sam celebrates birthday number sixteen!

So, as the three sat around the campsite that weekend, Sam eagerly blew out the candles on his birthday cake. Excited by the camping trip and his birthday adventure, Sam almost forgot his other wish until Brian fetched a small box from the back of the big purple truck. Sam jumped, clapped his hands, and rushed toward the box faster than Brian could gently remove the tiny kitten. Only a few weeks old, the little fur ball was solid black, except for a white spot on her nose. Wriggling free from Brian, she pounced into Sam's waiting arms.

The bonding was immediate!

Sam stroked the kitten, held her tightly and listened to the rhythm of her soft purr. In only a few minutes she burrowed beneath Sam's chin and fell asleep.

"She's all mine?" Sam questioned. "You promise?"

Lynn assured Sam that the kitten was truly his very own. As his eyes danced with delight, the inevitable question was raised.

"What are you going to name the kitten, Sam?"

He wrinkled his brow in deep four-year-old concentration. The name needed to be special, not just a predictable cat name. The kitten needed a name that would remind Sam of this special birthday. And, of course, it had to be a name everyone would easily remember.

Looking in all directions for inspiration, Sam suddenly spied a stack of wood Brian had split for their campfire. He flashed a huge dimpled grin.

"Firewood!" he shouted.

"Firewood? What are you talking about?" Brian asked.

"I'm talking about my kitten," Sam replied matter-of-factly. "I'm going to name her Firewood."

Brian and Lynn looked at each other with amusement. You know what they were thinking, of course: *"Firewood? What a crazy name! You will not name your cat Firewood."*

Though they may have thought Firewood was a crazy name for a cat, they never said it. Sam is lucky to have great parents who decided that their son could name his kitten anything he wanted. And who is to say that Firewood is not an absolutely magnificent name for a cat, anyway? It is definitely not an ordinary cat name and it will forever remind Sam of his fourth birthday and the camping trip he shared with his mom and dad.

From that day forward, a cat named Firewood was part of the Stinson household. Sam and Firewood wrestled together, watched television together, even slept together. Sometimes they would play outside until almost dark and Sam could hardly see the solid black cat with the white spot on her nose.

> **From that day forward, a cat named Firewood was part of the Stinson household.**

But when it was time to go inside for a good night's sleep, Sam would call his cat by name.

"Firewood! Firewood! Time to go inside."

And no matter where she was in the neighborhood, the little black fur ball with the white spot on her nose ran swiftly to her four-year-old Master. Scooping Firewood into his arms, Sam took her inside to rest for the night.

Sam never thought Firewood was a silly name for a cat. I like to think that Firewood was quite proud of her name. She was Firewood, Sam Stinson's kitten. And Firewood was always happiest when she heard her master calling her by name.

Cathy Lee Phillips

....

A kitten is the most irresistible comedian in the world. Its wide-open eyes gleam with wonder and mirth. It darts madly at nothing at all, and then, as though suddenly checked in the pursuit, prances sideways on its hind legs with ridiculous agility and zeal.

Agnes Repplier

Cats regard people as warmblooded furniture.

Jacquelyn Mitchard

....

L.A. BLUES

I was thrilled when my husband, Scott, announced he'd been transferred and we'd be moving from Kansas City to Los Angeles. I saw L.A. as an exciting city, full of fascinating if somewhat intimidating people. We found an apartment on the beach with a view of the ocean. While my husband put in long hours at his new job, I explored the area, looking forward to meeting my new neighbors.

I hardly had a chance. People flew by on Rollerblades, chillin' to the music on headsets instead of stopping to chat. It certainly wasn't the slow, friendly pace of Kansas City I was used to. The sun was a pale orange disk through the pollution, and cars clotted the freeways. I got a marketing job at one of the movie studios, but my coworkers seemed more interested in their careers than being friends with me. Disillusionment settled over me like, well, the smog. Scott had to travel for long stretches at a time on business, and increasingly I found myself all alone in Los Angeles. After work I went straight home. *Why try to make friends with these people?* I figured.

One Saturday as I was heading out on an errand, I saw a group of children huddled by the oleanders outside our building. Peering out between the thick, leathery leaves was a striped gray cat. "Here, kitty, kitty," one little girl said as she knelt and reached out her hand.

"Don't get too close!" a neighbor yelled from his deck. "He's nasty. He'll bite." Sure enough, the cat hissed and lashed out, sending the children scurrying.

I looked reproachfully at the man who had yelled. "That cat is wild," he informed me. "He's been living in those bushes, eating scraps and whatever else." Well, I knew cats. And I knew that cats generally gave as good as they got. A few days later I heard two kids tease him as they braked their bikes on the sandy sidewalk. "Hey, Bruno!" they taunted and got a hiss from him. *So he has a name.* The next time I walked by his bush, I called, "Bruno, Bruno."

He replied with his trademark hiss. *He probably feels out of place too,* I decided. My own back went up later when I heard one of the neighbors shout, "I'm going to kill that cat!" I had to help Bruno. He needed a home and he needed it now.

The one thing Bruno understood was food. I bought some kitty tuna, put it on our deck in a bowl and caught him nibbling furtively. The next day he was back again, gobbling what I'd put out but darting off when I got too close. Each day I moved the dish closer to our door, talking quietly to him. One day I reached out and gave him a scratch behind his ears. He arched his back and hissed, then went back to eating. At leasts he didn't run off.

A week or two later, when I moved the dish onto our living room floor, Bruno cautiously ventured inside to get his dinner. I kept talking as I pulled the front door shut, then sat on the floor. "Welcome to your new home, Bruno," I announced.

To my surprise, he took right away to life indoors even though he made himself scarce. As soon as I came home from work, he would scamper under the bed. It was a little like living with a phantom cat. I put out food in the living room, then watched from around the corner as he ate it up.

After about three months, Bruno began to come out of his shell. If I sat very still he let me stroke his back without trying to bite me. "You'll be okay here," I assured him one evening. "Nobody will hurt you." At the same time I began to resent the neighbors even more. Why hadn't they helped him? Why hadn't people showed they cared? Typical.

One night Bruno wouldn't eat. The next night, the same thing. What was wrong? Before long, his eyes and skin beneath his fur started looking yellow. Maybe he needs some vitamins. I mixed some into his food. He wouldn't touch it. I didn't relish the thought of taking him to the vet, but clearly it was time. I got a pet carrier and lured Bruno inside with some catnip, then took him off to an animal clinic. "We'll keep him for the night," said the woman at the desk, "so we can run some tests."

The veterinarian called me the next day. "Bruno has fatty liver disease," he said. "He's not able to absorb nutrients from his food. The humane thing to do is euthanize him."

"I have to think about this," I said. I got Bruno and brought him back to the apartment. When I let him out of the carrier, he actually curled up in my lap and purred. He was glad to be home.

"Please, God," I prayed, "don't let Bruno die." Scott was on business in China, but I called him there and asked him to pray for Bruno too. By the time I hung up, I was practically in tears. I'd had to telephone halfway around the world to find a caring voice.

The next day at work I got a call. "Hi, Lisa," a man said. "I'm a colleague of Scott's in the L.A. office. When he checked in this morning, he told me about your cat. I have a suggestion."

Someone in Los Angeles actually cared? "There's a great holistic clinic not far from you," he continued. "They do acupuncture there. Why don't you try it?" I explained that Bruno would hardly let anyone touch him, much less poke him with needles. "But I really appreciate your calling," I said. "It was nice of you."

I found another vet who came up with the same diagnosis— but a different plan of action.

The call made me realize I needed to get a second opinion on Bruno. I found another vet who came up with the same diagnosis— but a different plan of action. "No, you don't need to put him to sleep," he said. "He's not suffering. There's still hope."

The doctor inserted a tube in Bruno's neck so I could feed and medicate him at home. Every day after work I spent hours feeding Bruno through his tube. I had to help him. He was the only friend I had.

After Scott returned from China he pitched in, but nonetheless the stress was taking its toll on me. One morning a colleague said, "You okay, Lisa? You look tired." I started telling him about Bruno. People stopped by my cubicle to listen. Soon they were offering advice and sharing their own pet traumas. The next day a blond I'd once dismissed as being straight out of *Baywatch* brought me some catnip. "I'll put Bruno in my prayers too," she promised.

One night Bruno grew so weak I rushed him to an animal hospital emergency room at three o'clock in the morning.

Even in the middle of the night the waiting room was filled with cats, rabbits, birds, dogs, reptiles and their owners. A German shepherd limped over to inspect Bruno, but Bruno couldn't muster a hiss. "What are you here for?" the dog's owner asked, and we had one of those heart-to-heart talks about the ailments of our pets.

I noticed the other people in the waiting room nodding their heads in understanding. They looked just like the people I saw rushing by on the sidewalk and zooming past my car on the freeway. Had I really given L.A. a chance on its own terms? Had I been the one in too much of a hurry—a hurry to judge my new neighbors?

The vet treated Bruno with an IV and then sent us home. Gradually Bruno started to gain weight, and bit by bit he regained his old swagger. But he was a different Bruno. Less fearful, kinder, a little more willing to trust. Now when the vet and the workers in the clinic put out a hand to pet him, Bruno actually allowed a caress and purred.

The day the vet removed his feeding tube was cause for great celebration. My new friends at work sent home a huge canister of fancy gourmet cat snacks for him. That afternoon I held Bruno in my arms on our apartment steps and we sat there looking at the ocean. The warm sun poured through the palm trees as rollerbladers streaked past, and every once in a while someone would stop to admire my cat.

"May I pet him?" one little boy asked.

"Not yet," I said. "He's still getting used to strangers. But he's getting better."

And so was I.

Lisa Huntress

....

A dog, I have always said, is prose; a cat is a poem.

Jean Burden

....

"I have a couple of other projects I'm excited about."

I'M AN ANIMAL RESCUER

I am an Animal Rescuer
By the love of those who I've been privileged to
    rescue
I have been rescued.
I know what true unconditional love really is
For I've seen it shining in the eyes of so many

Grateful for so little.
I am an Animal Rescuer.
My work is never done.
My home is never quiet.
My wallet is always empty.
But my heart is always full.

Author Unknown

••

I know, when people see a cat's litter box, they always say, "Oh, have you got a cat?" Just once I want to say, "No, it's for company!"

Clever Magazine

A man who hated his wife's cat decided to get rid of it. He drove 20 blocks from home and let the cat go. But when he returned home, the cat was sitting in the driveway.

The next day the man decided to drop the cat 40 blocks away, but the exact same thing happened again.

The 3rd day he drove 10 miles away, turned left, went past a bridge, made 2 rights, 3 lefts, crossed some railroad tracks, and made another right before he stopped and scooted the cat out of the car.

Hours later, the man called his wife. "Jen, do you see the cat?"

"Yes. Why?"

"Put that cat on the phone," he said in frustration.

"I need directions back home."

Jim Kraus

A farmer is milking his cow and as he is milking, a fly comes along and flies into the cow's ear. A little bit later, the farmer notices the fly in the milk. The farmer says, "Hmph. In one ear, out the udder."

Prairie Home Companion

Feline Frustration, Rule of. When your cat has fallen asleep on your lap and looks utterly content and adorable, you will suddenly have to go to the bathroom.

Donald R. Woods

MIDNIGHT VISITORS

When my husband was transferred to Palmdale, California, homes were hard to find, so we were shown a place in the nearby foothills. But no one told us the knotty-pine cabin was more holes than knots. Or that little wild creatures had already laid claim to it.

I had just driven back from taking the kids to the school bus stop and opened the kitchen door, when a furry little animal streaked across the linoleum floor. "Aha!" I yelled. "So you're the fellow that was banging around in my pan cupboards last night!" I didn't relish being kept awake, or rewashing pots and skillets at five in the morning. In fact, I resented any critter, animal or human, who imposed upon me.

That was one reason I had welcomed moving to the country. In Pasadena, because I had three young boys in school and two little ones at home, I'd been elected neighborhood chauffeur and baby-sitter. The gals reasoned that since I had so many kids of my own, a few more wouldn't make any difference. But they did. My own five I could cope with, but add three or four in the station wagon and a dozen in the yard, and things invariably got out of hand. But instead of talking out and working out the problems with my neighbors, I retreated to a position of resentment and isolation. I felt they were taking advantage of me.

When my husband brought home the news of his transfer to the high desert, it actually came as a welcome relief. And our move to the foothills was even more appealing, for as I looked down the road, there wasn't a neighbor in sight.

That evening at supper I told my husband we'd have to do something about the little pack rats. "I'll bait a trap," he promised. But with that, the boys set up a howl. They, too, had caught a glimpse of these bright-eyed, big-eared creatures and loved them on sight. "Our own Mickey Mouses," four-year-old Tim chortled.

"Yeah!" his brothers yelled. "Can't we keep 'em for pets, Daddy?"

"Pets!" I cried. "You mean pests, and no way will I live with them!"

They appealed to their dad, but he said, "You heard your mother."

Still, we understood how they felt, for they missed their collie that had been run over by a car just before we moved. So their dad waited until they were asleep before setting the trap. The next morning the bait was untouched. Again I had to wash all the pots and pans. And when I started to pull on my boots, I couldn't get into them until I poured out a handful of peanut shells. "Now I know why they didn't take the bait," I grumbled to my husband. That night I cleared all the snack food off the kitchen counter and crammed it into the refrigerator.

But the following morning, unbelievable as it seemed, the cheese was still in the trap. Grimly I rewashed the pans. Later, when I went to the clothes closet, I found pink feathers all over the floor! The mischievous pests had chewed all the trim off my hat. But surely, I thought, they must be getting hungry by now. Unless . . . Suspicion crossed my mind. "I'll bet that's it!" I muttered. That night, before bed, I pulled up the tablecloth and looked underneath. Sure enough, I swept up a dustpanful of bread scraps and peanuts the boys had dropped on the floor for our pack-rat visitors.

But losing their food supply didn't stop them. It made them malicious: They clattered and banged around worse than ever that night. And by morning the whole house was strewn with paper clips, buttons, keys, spoons, socks—anything small enough for them to tote. "Okay," I yelled at the culprit who went skittering across the kitchen in broad daylight, "this is it! Beat it and don't come back!" And with that I picked up a book and threw it at him.

I guess he got the message. We didn't see him or any of his

buddies for the next couple of days. What a relief! No more sleepless nights and no more pans to wash before breakfast. But the worst was yet to come.

Perhaps it was the rustling sound—or the click of tiny toenails on linoleum—but I awoke with a start even before the alarm went off that morning. I turned on the light and looked around. Then I shook my husband awake. "Have you seen my wristwatch?"

"Umph," he grunted, then mumbled, "Go back to sleep."

"Wake up!" I insisted. "I know I left it right there on the nightstand, and now it's gone!"

That got through to him: "Oh-oh," he said. "I'm just remembering. A guy at work said pack rats are also called trade rats. It's their nature to carry things around, but they're always on the lookout for something more attractive to swap for."

"Like my shiny wristwatch!" I exclaimed. Then I moaned, "It was the first good watch I ever owned!"

"I know," he sympathized. Then with a wry twist to his mouth, he asked, "And what did the crook leave you for it?"

I couldn't stand to look again, so I pointed over my shoulder at the nightstand—where lay a bright aluminum bottle cap.

After searching the whole house, we figured this scoundrel had carried the watch outside to his huge wigwam-shaped stick nest to hoard it. Had there been only one nest, I would have torn it apart stick by stick but there were dozens of them close by. In the meantime, the night raids continued, until we didn't feel safe to lay any small thing down. I was at my wit's end.

Finally I cried, "Help, Lord!" I was ashamed of turning to Him now, for I hadn't prayed much since I developed my standoffish feelings about neighbors. I knew I didn't deserve His help, and I wasn't even sure He'd heard me. Nevertheless, something hap-

I knew I didn't deserve His help, and I wasn't even sure He'd heard me.

pened that afternoon that made me wonder. Waiting at the bus stop to pick up the boys, I met another mother who acted so friendly I couldn't help but respond. Then, letting my guard down a bit, I found myself telling her my troubles.

"What you need," she said, "is a good cat. I've got one I could let you have."

"How much?" I asked, suspiciously.

"Nothing. I'll give her to you."

"Oh, I don't know . . ." I said. Probably she had a whole barn full and just wanted to get rid of one.

"She'll keep the pack rats away, and even other varmints."

Still I hesitated. Then I thought, What's the matter with me? She only wants to help. So I said, "I'll take her! And Thanks!" We both smiled, and my icy attitude began to melt.

The boys were overjoyed at having a real pet again. They named the big white cat Snowball and helped me bed her down in the kitchen. During the night I awakened and thought of Snowball prowling around on her velvet pads, ready to pounce. I dreaded hearing a squeal. But everything was quiet. I wondered if she'd let us down.

No so. The next morning the pan cupboard was still clean, and the whole house was neat. I seems it had taken only the smell of a feline to send the little pack rats scurrying back to where they came from. How simple, I thought, and how natural. But that's the way the Lord usually works. Like leading me to a woman who showed me that neighbors need each other—and that simple communication can cure all kinds of problems. "Thank You, Lord," I said, "I needed to learn this lesson."

And now, He asked, don't you think it's time you forgave your old neighbors?

"Oh yes, Lord. It's the least I can do when I think of the countless times You've forgiven me."

Snowball was standing by the kitchen door, so I let her out and poured her a bowl of milk. And when she'd finished it, she rubbed her sleek white head against my jean leg and began to purr.

For the next few months, just by occupying the back porch, Snowball scared away lizards, gophers, rabbits, squirrels and snakes. We thought we had made it. Then one day I opened the door to find her hobnobbing with a varmint so scary I froze in my tracks. What was the matter with her? Didn't she recognize this plumed black-and-white creature for what he was?

"I can't believe it!" I squeaked, backing away and closing the door softly. First pack rats, and now a skunk! Then something about the situation rang a bell. Another lesson? "Oh, no, Lord!" I cried.

But that's another story.

Laverne Riley O'Brien

• •

It is impossible to keep a straight face in the presence of one or more kittens.

Cynthia E. Varnado

• •

6

Tales of Tails and Snails

It's amazing what kinds of unusual pets and animals people love as companions, isn't it? And yet, their stories are as fascinating as those about "ordinary" pets. Is there such a thing as an "ordinary" pet anyway? Not to the people who call them friends.

CAESAR, BRUTUS, AND ST. FRANCIS

I'm taking you guys to church, so please try to behave, okay?" Our two rambunctious young beagles, Caesar and Brutus, sat on the front seat of the car and ignored me, their floppy ears perked to attention as they watched the stream of traffic. At the stoplight, I braked as a woman walked her black poodle across the street. Caesar and Brutus let out a string of woo-woo-woofs.

"Now see? That's what I mean," I told them. "None of that."

It was a balmy October afternoon and we were on our way to a "Blessing of the Animals" service at Grace Episcopal

Church. I'd never attended one of these services, and frankly, I had no idea what to expect. I only knew it was held each year on St. Francis Day (since St. Francis had a special love for animals) and that folks were invited to bring their pets. From the moment I'd read about it, I'd had a nudging feeling I should go.

Now I wondered if I was out of my mind. What if Caesar and Brutus disrupted the service? It would be just like them. Beagles are bred to do three things: sniff, bark, and charge at anything furry. Once my son found Caesar in our fenced backyard stranded up in a crepe myrtle tree where he'd climbed after a squirrel.

Earlier in the day I'd asked my children if they would like to come along to see the dogs blessed. "Let me get this straight," said Bob. "You're taking our dogs to church to get blessed with a lot of other animals?" He was biting the inside of his mouth to keep from laughing. Ann had simply gazed at me with her when-are-you-checking-into-the-asylum look.

I looked at the dogs, thumping their tails on the car seat, barking at everything that moved outside the car. "Will you be quiet?" I cried. The truth is, I'd never taken to these two hyperactive beagles the way I had to our beloved old, slow-moving spaniel, Captain. He'd presided quietly over the house for 13 years before he died. These two were his so-called "replacements." Some replacements.

I turned into the church parking lot just as the service was about to begin. Beside the children's playground was a table draped in white with a St. Francis statue on it. A little crescent of children, adults, dogs (quiet dogs), and other animals had formed around it. I lashed Caesar's and Brutus's leashes to my wrists like a rodeo cowboy getting ready to ride into the ring.

The dogs came out of the car in a yapping frenzy, noses to the ground, dragging me behind them. I tugged and wrestled them over to the other animals. The priest was saying something about celebrating the presence of animals on earth, how they too were part of God's wonderful plan.

"Woo-woo-woof! Woo-woo-woof!" they barked and bayed at the other dogs, drowning out the voice of the priest. People looked at me and smiled sympathetically. Even the other dogs stared at me.

Caesar and Brutus then spotted a pet carrier on the ground to my left. Sitting regally behind the wire was a cat. "Woo-woo-woof!" They lunged toward the cat, nearly tipping me over. The priest was practically shouting now. I frantically tried to hush them as they strained on their leashes, which were cutting into my wrists to the point of pain. *Lord, what a disaster!* I thought. My children were right. This was a dumb idea. Just wait till I get you two home. I wanted to leave, but something—I don't know what—held me there.

The priest moved from one animal to the next, patting their heads, saying something to each one. Finally he stopped in front of my two dis-turbers of the peace and asked their names. "Caesar and Brutus," I replied in the most apolo-getic tone possible.

He touched their heads and smiled. "Bless you, Caesar and Brutus. We're thankful for your enthu-siasm about life, for the joyful noise you make in response to it. May God watch over you and pro-tect you."

Next we read in unison the famous prayer of St. Francis, our words filtering through the aria of my dogs' unending barking: "Lord, make me an instrument of Thy peace . . ."

Finally, mercifully, it was over.

Back home I opened the gate, let Caesar and Brutus into the backyard, then trudged into the kitchen muttering.

The priest moved from one animal to the next, patting their heads, saying something to each one.

"What happened?" asked my husband, Sandy.

"Those fool dogs practically ruined the St. Francis Day service. They acted like animals."

"They are animals," he pointed out.

For days I refused to let them in the house, where they usually slept. I scolded them for the least thing: for the limbs they dragged onto the deck, for turning over my Boston fern, for scratching at the door, but mostly for barking. They responded by wagging their tails and dropping a ball in front of me, hoping I would toss it. I would not.

Five days after the St. Francis Day disaster I happened to glance out the window and see the neighbor's cat sashaying along the back fence. An eerie feeling came over me. Why weren't the dogs barking? I stepped into the yard, into an awful, empty silence. With a thudding heart I peered at the gate. It was hanging open. Caesar and Brutus were gone.

I ran down the driveway, remembering Sandy's caution to keep the gates closed. "If those two dogs ever get out, I'm afraid they'll be long gone," he'd said. Had the meter reader come through and left it ajar? Had the wind blown it open?

I hurried along the street calling their names. After scouring the neighborhood for two hours, I came home. There had been no sign of them. They had probably seen a squirrel and tracked it clear to North Carolina by now.

Sandy came home during lunch and we drove all over town. "If we ever find them, I'll never fuss at them again," I told Sandy.

He smiled at me. "I know."

After school the children joined the search. Late into the afternoon I kept stopping people on the street. "Have you seen two little beagles?" They all shook their heads.

As the day softened into dusk, we gave up and went home. I passed their dog bowls sitting empty in the kitchen and walked on into my study. I sat alone in the shadows and traced my finger along the edge of my desk. Suddenly I remembered how the priest put his hands on their heads. What had he said? "Bless you, Caesar and Brutus. We're thankful for your enthusiasm for life. . . . May God watch over you and protect you." I laid my head down and cried.

When I dried my eyes, it was dark out. I stood at the window and wondered if we would ever see them again. Just then part of St. Francis's prayer came floating back into my head: ". . . Where there is doubt, let me sow faith; where there is despair, hope . . ." The words seemed full of urgency. I grabbed a flashlight and both dog leashes and headed out the door.

"Where are you going?" Sandy asked.

"To sow faith and hope," I said.

I walked along the street, on and on, block after block.

"Woo-woo-woof!"

I froze. I would know that sound anywhere. I listened, following it until I came upon Caesar and Brutus sniffing through the garden in a stranger's yard. In the middle of the garden was a statue of St. Francis. Somehow I was not surprised.

As the dogs bounded into my arms and licked my face, I thanked God for St. Francis, who loved all creatures great and small, and was still teaching folks today to do the same. I thanked God for blessing my two beagles and for watching over them.

Back home I gave both dogs some milk and let them curl up on the foot of my bed. I rubbed their ears. Feeling that great and piercing awareness that breaks in upon us at certain times in life, the awareness of not realizing how much you love the people or things close to you until you almost lose them.

I was suddenly filled with the need to seize every day and sow it full of all those wonderful things St. Francis prayed about: love and pardon, faith and hope, light and joy.

Sandy and the children appeared at the bedroom door. I went and put my arms around them. "I don't tell you enough," I said, "but I love you."

From the foot of the bed came a resounding, "Woo-woo-woof."

Sue Monk Kidd

MAKING ROOM

A seeing eye dog boarded a crowded streetcar and led his master to the only available space—a small gap on the seat that ran the length of the car. The space was too small for an adult, but the dog began nudging with his nose the people on either side. They moved farther apart, and their neighbors squeezed against one another until the empty space was large enough for two people. The dog then nudged his master, signaling him to be seated. The passengers broke into laughter as the dog climbed up into the space beside the blind man and relaxed with his head on his master's lap.

Rusty Wright and Linda Raney Wright

CANINE LIMITS

Don't say that nothin' is impossible until you've tried to teach your dog to eat an artichoke.

Michael Hodgin

Some scientist spent twenty years in the lab inventing ice cream for dogs. He made it taste like vanilla, so it's hardly selling at all. If he'd made it taste like doody, dogs would be robbing stores with guns.

Elayne Boosler

THE FAMILY CIRCUS®   By Bil Keane

"I like dogs 'cause if you're doing something stupid,
they don't yell at you. They do it with you."

DOGS AND PEOPLE ARE MUCH ALIKE!

If you're under 50, you probably don't remember the famous ad featuring "Nipper," the little white dog with his head cocked and black ears alert, sitting on his haunches beside an old gramophone with a huge, brass horn "speaker" on top. The accompanying slogan, "Listening for His Master's Voice," was equally famous.

It had been years since I'd thought of Nipper . . . until he suddenly came to mind the other day while I was waiting in the car until my husband completed an errand. That's when I noticed an intently-waiting/listening, Nipper-looking terrier rooted to the sidewalk, outside a builder's supply.

Now probably a hundred customers went in and out of those doors, but that little dog ignored all of them. Obviously, his attention was focused on one person only, and I began hoping Lawrence's return would be delayed so I could see just who that person was and what would happen when he/she finally did appear.

The dog's delight left no doubt whom he'd been waiting for when just then, a husky, middle-aged man emerged, with a sack of potting soil on one shoulder and a couple of wooden planks on the other. If dogs can laugh, this one did—his tongue lolling in a wide-open mouth while he jumped, pogo like, in circles around his master. He happily trotted alongside and impatiently paced until sack and lumber were safely stoewed in the pickup's bed. Then he leaped into the truck, gave his owner's right ear a few licks, and finally flopped on the seat—apparently content just in being with the one he adored.

Isabel Wolseley Torrey

•••

So, these vultures decided to fly to Florida on an airline. They got on board carrying six dead raccoons, and the flight attendant said, "I'm sorry, but there's a limit of two carrion per passenger."

Prairie Home Companion

•••

WELCOME, DOG

A man who planned a vacation in Colorado hardly knew what to do with his dog. So he wrote the motel and asked if he could bring a dog. The motel manager wrote back:

"For 25 years I've been in this business. Never has a dog been careless with a cigarette and set fire to the bed. Never have I found a motel towel or blanket in a dog's suitcase. Nor have I ever found a whisky ring on a dresser caused by a dog's leaving a bottle on it. Furthermore, never have I called the police to evict a disorderly dog. We welcome the dog and if he will vouch for you, you may come along with him."

Leroy Brownlow

••

The duck walks into a drugstore and he says, "Gimme some Chapstick and put it on my bill."

Prairie Home Companion

••

How to Photograph Your Puppy

Remove film from box and load camera.

Remove film box from puppy's mouth and throw in trash.

Remove puppy from trash and brush coffee grounds from muzzle.

Choose a suitable background for photo.

Mount camera on tripod, check flash, and focus.

Find puppy and take dirty sock from mouth.

Place puppy in prefocused spot and return to camera.

Forget about spot and crawl after puppy on knees.

Focus with one hand while fending off puppy with other hand.

Get tissue and clean nose print from lens.

Put cat outside and put peroxide on the scratch on puppy's nose.

Put magazines back on coffee table.

Try to get puppy's attention by squeaking toy over your head.

Replace your glasses and check camera for damage.

Jump up in time to grab puppy by scruff of neck and say, "No, no outside!"

Call spouse to help clean up the mess.

Fix a drink.

Sit back in chair, put your feet up, sip your drink and resolve to teach puppy "sit" and "stay" first thing in the morning.

Dog Haus

THE LITTLE PUPPY THAT COULD

R unt of the litter, he was. With his red-brown coloring and dark eyes, he was a beautiful miniature of whatever mixture his mother was. Obviously the "love 'em and leave 'em" type, neither the identity nor lineage of his father was ever discovered. The tiny pup was the smallest of six born in a dark corner beneath the house on Posey Road.

The underneath of our house was quite a popular birthing place for various dogs and cats that populated Posey Road. It was cool, dark, and virtually inaccessible to humans—except for young tomboys undaunted by whatever creeping and crawling creatures shared the space. When the house became quiet at night I often listened for the unmistakable soft squeaks of newborn puppies or kittens lying next to their mother in an isolated corner beneath the house. When I heard these sounds I could hardly wait for daylight and the chance to locate the newest residents of Posey Road.

This particular autumn night, I heard the familiar squeak

and before breakfast the next morning, I had crawled under the house and found a mother dog carefully guarding six newborn furry puppies. When I first saw the tiniest of the litter, he quickly captured my heart. Okay, I am a sucker for the underdog, and I watched as this little one fought his way toward his mother and her abundant food supply. I also watched as his five bigger and equally hungry siblings pushed him to the back of the line. But with dogged determination, this scrappy little one fought his way back to the source of nourishment. Though he received sustenance, he remained smaller than his other four-legged siblings.

The puppies remained secluded during their first few weeks. As their eyes opened and they grew stronger, they crawled from beneath the house and explored the outside world.

This dog remained the smallest, but he was tough and strong for his size. Because of his strength and his thick furry hair, I called him Samson. I thought the name fit him well, though there were some who snickered at this small runt of a puppy sharing the name of the strong man of the Old Testament. But the puppy had gumption, stamina, resourcefulness, and yes, guts. He had learned to fend for himself and that life did not promise him any favors.

So it was that Samson became a well-known, albeit, petite member of the Posey Road citizenry. He made his place in the world and never caused a problem until the day he caught sight of the hog's head.

Dare I call it "puppy love" at first sight?

The hog's head was a by-product of butchering that had taken place earlier in the day. Several families had gathered to, delicately stated, *convey* two pigs from the pen to the freezer. This "conveyance" is hard work and usually a full day is dedicated to butchering one pig.

This group, though, felt that two pigs could be butchered, gutted, and prepared for the freezer if we began before daybreak. Thus, the process began one cold morning and by mid-afternoon, the procedure was well underway.

The preparation of Brunswick Stew was a regular part of the day's activity. While there are many variations on the classic Brunswick Stew recipe, ours included using meat from the hog's head as the essential ingredient of the stew. Normal procedure involved boiling the aforementioned head in a black cauldron over an open fire. When the steam began rising from the pot on a cold day, it appeared as though a smelly witches brew was a'simmering on Posey Road. The objective was to boil the head until the tender meat fell off the head, leaving behind only a few naked bones and a set of clenched teeth.

I do admit that the procedure may sound a bit gory and those of you unaccustomed to this way of life may need to pause and quickly guzzle a bottle of Pepto Bismol. Nevertheless, the finished product was the perfect blend of a tomato base with meat and vegetables that warmed both the stomach and the heart on a cold frosty evening.

This day, however, presented one slight dilemma—there were two hog's heads yet only one black pot. Obviously, only one head could be boiled at a time. Thus, the first head was cleaned and thrust into the huge dark kettle. Four to five hours later Mama pronounced the head "done" and two men removed it and set it to cool on a wooden table next to the fire.

Though you may still be feeling a bit queasy, Samson—runt of the litter—was intrigued and inexplicably drawn to the unique aroma of a freshly boiled hog's head. While his brothers and sisters scrounged for food in other directions, this little guy decided the hog's head would be a virtual daylong feast for him! So when everyone's attention was diverted, the runt Samson hopped up, placed his paws on the wooden table, and wrestled this very large hog's head to the ground. He tugged and pulled at the fresh meat, rolling the head in the grass and dirt as he gnawed away at the goods.

Samson was well involved in his feasting before Aunt Zelma observed the little puppy chewing on this very large porcine skull, quite literally making a "pig" of himself. Grabbing a large metal spoon, she promptly chased Samson away from the head. Reluctant to leave his treasure, Aunt Zelma had to whack Samson a couple of times before he relinquished his feast and retreated to his hideaway beneath the house. As he made his exit, the dog left behind one seriously revolting hog's head with semi-naked bones and clenched teeth covered with a nauseating combination of grass, dirt, and assorted dog germs.

Now, I must admit that, even on Posey Road, there were limits to the consumption of a hog's head, and it took only seconds to deduce that this particular head was certainly not stew-worthy.

Next question? What was one to do with the, uh, remains? What would Miss Manners say was the proper means of disposing of one boiled, half-eaten hog's head with semi-naked bones, clenched teeth, covered with a nauseating combination of grass, dirt, and assorted dog germs?

Like a soldier on a covert operation in wartime, Samson followed the truck without being detected.

Solution? The Posey Road pond. Two men lifted the object, loaded it onto the back of a truck, and set out for the pond located about one mile from the house.

Like a soldier on a covert operation in wartime, Samson followed the truck without being detected.

The men drove to the pond and, arriving at what they deemed a fitting site, they lifted the remains from the back of the truck and threw the hog's head into the pond with all their force. Though these were strong men, the weight of the head kept it from going very far from the edge of the pond. But, satisfied with the committal, the men returned to the task of dressing the second hog.

Meanwhile, Samson returned to his own task.

Well over an hour later, Aunt Zelma herself broke into an eerie fit of laughter. Looking up, the approximately 20 adults joined in the gawking and laughing as the meager Samson, runt of the litter, appeared at the edge of the yard, awkwardly struggling with one very large, very wet, very repulsive pig's head. With sheer "pig-headed" determination, that little dog had summoned all his strength to jump into the edge of the pond, pull the hog's head from the water, and drag it back home to complete the feast he had started earlier that afternoon. What a spectacle! The skeletal remains virtually eclipsed the tiny but determined creature that would not be deterred from enjoying his gourmet meal of freshly boiled hog's head.

Amazingly, Samson suddenly became quite popular with his five hypocritical siblings who quickly gathered around him, intent on sharing the fruits of his labor. Samson, however, seemed suddenly empowered and growled menacingly at his greedy siblings who backed away in astonishment.

No one, including Aunt Zelma, bothered Samson for the rest of the day. We left the little dog alone with his hog's head as he ate, chewed, licked and, finally, slept either from a full stomach or sheer exhaustion.

Runt of the litter, he was. He fought his way into the world and continued to fight for his place in the world. After lo these many years, I barely remember the other puppies in that litter, but I will never forget Samson.

Cathy Lee Phillips

MY DOG

His nose is short and scrubby;
His ears hang rather low;
And he always brings the stick back,
No matter how far you throw.

He gets spanked rather often
For things he shouldn't do,
Like lying on beds, and barking,
And eating up shoes when they're new.

He always wants to be going
Where he isn't supposed to go.
He tracks up the house when it's snowing—
Oh, puppy, I love you so.

Marchette Chute

"Since we're both being honest,
I should tell you I have fleas."

THE LION QUEEN

You never know when you're going to fall in love. For me, it happened in the summer of 1965 in a darkened movie theater. My mom had started a part-time job selling tickets there. On nights when Dad was able to look after my little brother, Ronnie, and the feature was appropriate for a ten-year-old, Mom would bring me to work. I'd sit up front with a box of popcorn in my lap and get carried away to a world far beyond the Chicago suburbs.

One evening the lights went down and I found myself looking at a sea of tall grass spreading to the horizon. I'd never seen a landscape like that before. But it felt instantly familiar, as familiar as my own backyard. A woman in a khaki bush jacket introduced herself as Joy Adamson. The movie—*Born Free*—told the story of the orphaned lion cub that she adopted, raised, and eventually returned to the wild.

Africa. I knew nothing about Africa. Yet I felt like I knew everything on some deeper level that was there for me to explore, like the continent itself. At home in bed I couldn't get the film's Serengeti landscapes out of my head. On the screen of my imagination I saw myself venture deep into that limitless wild world, staying out in the bush for weeks at a time, getting to know the animals that lived there. Especially the lions.

The next morning I made a critical decision: I cut my long hair short. It would be easier to keep clean when I was deep in the bush. Then I removed the green-and-blue checkered curtains from my bedroom windows. I put up new ones made from a zebra-stripe pattern I discovered in a fabric store. My pink T-shirts and floral pedal pushers were banished to the depths of my dresser, replaced by a safari vest and matching hat. I would definitely be ready when the time came.

The time would come. I knew it.

"What's the suitcase for, Janice?" my mom wanted to know, eyeing the small blue travel case open at the foot of my bed.

"Africa," I told her, surprised she couldn't figure it out. I was going to Africa one day. I knew it with a certitude that I'd never felt about anything else (except maybe for wanting to someday be a mom). I'd never wanted anything the way I wanted this. I wanted it so badly I was sure the Lord wanted it for me too.

I saved up for a set of LPs called *Learn Swahili* I saw advertised in a magazine. Night after night I'd practice my phrases until Ronnie shouted, *"Tulia!"*—Swahili for "shut up." Did I shut up? Nope. I'd just lower my voice and keep practicing.

Mom and Dad took my new passion in stride. But as the months passed and my fixation on trekking through the Serengeti only grew, Mom got a little nervous. Several years before Ronnie and I came along, our older sister Cynthia died of a heart condition. She'd been born with a large hole in her heart. Since I was five my doctor had been monitoring what he called an "innocent" murmur in my heart. "Innocent" or not, Mom was understandably extra protective of me.

Dad took me to the zoo in the hope that seeing a lion in the flesh might cure me of my African fever. It actually made it worse. The sight of that poor creature trapped behind the bars of a cage that read "Serengeti Lion" just made me more determined than ever to see a wild one. Would I ever be able to, though? I was frail, the doctor had said, and frail women didn't go tramping through the bush in search of lions. Born free? Not me.

Lord, I begged that night, kneeling against the bed where my blue travel case still lay open and waiting, please don't let this be the end of my dream.

And like a candle that can't be blown out, my obsession continued to burn. Yes, people thought I was odd. Did I care? Nope. I graduated high school in 1974 and landed my first job—filing checks in the basement of a bank. A year or so of working here, I calculated, and I'll save enough for a trip to Africa. Then, on Valentine's Day, Dad suffered a fatal coronary in the office of a doctor he was going to see about his own heart condition.

I stowed my little blue suitcase back in the closet. My Africa plans were on hold, so I could help Mom raise Ronnie.

Then it happened again—I fell in love. Not with a movie or a continent. This time it was Bob. We dated for only six weeks before he popped the question.

"So where do you think we should go on our honeymoon?" he asked. "I was thinking maybe . . . Africa."

"Oh, Bob. Do you really think we can?"

"Why not? It's always been your dream. Now that you're going to be my wife, it's my dream too. We're going to Africa and see real lions."

We scheduled an October wedding. I knew enough about Africa to know that fall is cool and pleasant—a perfect time to visit the Serengeti. With Bob with me I'd be safe. This was why the Lord had given me this incredible desire, then kept me waiting—for Bob.

I saw my doctor in August. He lingered longer than usual with the stethoscope on my chest. He was listening, listening intently. I wanted to pull away and not let him hear whatever it was he was hearing deep inside my heart. I knew it was bad.

"Janice," he said at last, "we're going to need to do some tests."

That "innocent" murmur? Turns out it wasn't so harmless after all. In fact I had a hole about the size of a half-dollar in my heart. The same condition my sister had died from.

Of course it made no difference to Bob. He said I had heart to spare. We went ahead with our wedding, but the Serengeti honeymoon didn't happen. The doctor said overseas travel was not advisable, especially the African bush where medical services were nonexistent. I thought of Mom and Ronnie and Bob. I owed it to them to take care of myself. I feared that meant giving up a dream as big as a continent and as alive as a lion, a dream I always believed was a gift from God. So I said the hardest prayer of my life. Lord, you put this dream into my heart. If it's not to be, change me so I can relinquish it.

And that other dream I had? Of being a mom? In 1982 Bob and I welcomed Sarah, the first of our two daughters adopted from South Korea, into our lives. Joy joined us in 1986. Nothing could have given me more joy. Not that I'd forgotten about Africa. All you needed to do was walk into our living room and see the drums and the big picture of a Serengeti lion hanging on the wall to know that.

But something was different now. It was okay if I never went to Africa. I had Africa in my heart. Ever since that night in the theater when I was ten, that dream had sustained me through my father's death and my own medical problems. It had been a light that brought me through darkness. That's why I had my dream. The Lord had given me so much that I wouldn't dare ask for more. I was content.

That night I joined Bob for dinner with a business associate of his and his wife. I mentioned my lifelong love of Africa and my dream to meet a wild lion face to face.

A few weeks later the phone rang. It was the wife of Bob's business associate. "Janice, do you still want to meet a lion? Because if you do, there's going to be one in my basement tomorrow."

A friend of hers worked with a wild animal sanctuary. She'd just called with a strange request. She was transporting a ten-week-old cub to the sanctuary, and they needed a place to stay for the night.

The next day, hand in hand with my two daughters, I walked down the stairs to the basement.

"Look, Mom," said Sarah. "There he is."

On a couch at the far end of the room was a small beige puff of fur with four absurdly large paws. I walked over and it was almost as if I was back in that long-ago theater stepping into the scene on the screen. The cub raised his head and looked at me with beautiful golden eyes, eyes I'd seen so

> I'd imagined Africa as an impossibly large place. Yet somehow I was holding it all in my arms.

many times in my mind that I knew them by heart. A sound came from his chest, a sound that would someday be a roar. It was like a purr, but deeper. All of Africa was inside it.

I sat down and held him in my arms. I'd imagined Africa as an impossibly large place. Yet somehow I was holding it all in my arms. I buried my face in his thick fur and breathed in. He had a wild smell, nothing like a dog or a domestic cat. It was a smell I would never forget. Who could have imagined that my safari could take place in a basement in Illinois?

The cub curled up. In a few seconds he was sound asleep. I sat there quietly, holding him and listening to his steady, slow breathing. The dream that I had nourished in my heart all these years had come true at last—in God's time, and in a way that only he could have imagined.

Janice Asien LaRosa

A VIEW FROM THE ZOO

I have listened to hundreds of zoo patrons say some incredible things about the animals, but none more incredible than what Henry told Mildred about the Beisa oryx. A Beisa oryx is an African antelope. It is one of the larger members of the family, standing about three and one-half feet at the shoulder. Its slender horns curve gracefully another two feet above the head. It is a combination of subtle gray, brown, black, and white—a strikingly beautiful animal.

Henry studied the oryx for several seconds. You could tell he was impressed. By the look of his clothing and the sound of his accent, my guess was that he was visiting from the

Ozarks of Arkansas. I couldn't be sure, but certainly he was from somewhere in the Deep South. His voice caught my attention. I was inside a barn talking to an animal keeper about a medication he would be giving one of the animals on his string when Henry began to lecture his family on what he had learned by reading the zoo sign. I peeked out the door and saw Henry surrounded by his three little boys. They were all dressed in overalls and wore no shirts. Mildred, his wife, stood where I would have stood if my family were dressed that way in Southern California—about twenty feet away. It didn't do any good, though, because he kept shouting some new particle of information he had gleaned from a sign.

"Hey, Mildred," he hollered, "you won't believe this! This here oryx has a gestation period of 267 days. That is a mighty long time to digest your food."

"What does it mean, Daddy?" ventured one of the cherubs.

"Billy Joe, it means that what this animal eats now won't be eliminated until next February." Then he smiled and said, "Ain't that amazing?"

It was mid July.

Gary Richmond

PLAYMATES

What a life our puppy leads
Filling his small owners' needs!
First he's wearing dolly clothes,
Then sporting specs upon his nose.
They fence him in with rocking chairs
And make him kneel to say his prayers;
They tie blue ribbons on his tail
Or make believe that he's in jail.
They put some booties on his feet
And serve him muddy pies to eat.

And through it all, he wags and licks
The little hands which play these tricks!

Mary Ellen Stelling

ASHLEY AT THE GATE

Four fulltime residents populated our home when my husband, Jerry, and I were married. Two cocker spaniels, Rhett and Ashley (Margaret Mitchell would be so proud!), rounded out the family. They couldn't have been more different. Ashley was coal-black, timid, and cautious. Reddish-blonde Rhett was a restless, terminally happy creature who loved to howl at night until Jerry broke this habit by applying Tabasco sauce to his tongue. Rhett, obviously an ADHD dog, needed doggie Ritalin to calm him. Ashley was more of a Prozac dog—in need of something to perk her up.

For years, these dogs lived inside a fence behind our home on Henderson Mill Road where their boundaries kept them safely away from passing Marta buses. Ashley was quite content but Rhett was ready to escape whenever the gate was opened even slightly.

As a United Methodist Minister, Jerry was involved in one of those well-known moves one June. We were moving to a rural church which would be quite a change for all of us, including Rhett and Ashley. There was no fence at our new location and because they were *city dogs*, we felt it best to build a barrier to keep them away from the brisk traffic on Highway 20 between Canton and Cumming.

The back yard was a beautiful vast green pasture with ample room for a fence of any size. Jerry observed the location, cogitated a bit, made measurements and created the outline of a fine fence. He bought necessary supplies, including a metal gate identical to the one we left at the house on Henderson Mill Road.

Several friends and church members volunteered to help assemble this fence one Saturday.

"We will put up the gate first and then build the fence to meet it on both sides," they explained to me.

Whatever, I thought. I was a fence-building rookie.

On fence-building day, we released the dog leashes and urged Rhett and Ashley to explore their new domain. Ashley experienced a doggie meltdown! She trembled, her eyes glazed over and she couldn't move. Rhett, meanwhile, rolled in every blade of grass on the property and enjoyed every minute of his freedom.

The building began. As holes were dug and the gate set in place, Ashley ran toward my lap. In the distance, Rhett happily performed back flips and ran in circles. As stakes were hammered into the ground, Ashley rolled over so I could rub her tummy, her eyes closed with delight. Rhett chased a large monarch butterfly, jumping, twisting, and yapping at the flying creature. When fencing was unrolled, Ashley jumped nervously. Rhett, meanwhile, discovered the nearby creek and engaged in about 30 minutes of splashing, barking, and playing before extracting himself from the cool water. Wet, matted and dripping, he looked at me as if he had discovered heaven. I could swear that the dog was smiling! Ashley looked up momentarily and rolled her eyes as if to say, *"What a crazy dog!"* (These are my interpretations—Ashley and I never actually conversed.)

When she looked up, Ashley spied a comforting sight. The gate was in place—standing tall, secure, and reassuring. Moving slowly, she marched to the gate, circled, sniffed and examined it closely. I could swear the dog was smiling! With a sigh, she plopped herself down on the inside of the gate— the same side of the gate she had been looking through for years at our home in the city. Her trembling slowed. Workers stopped to watch the dog that, in the midst of change, discovered security in her customary spot behind the gate. The fence, of course, had not been completed and limitations existed only in Ashley's mind. But those boundaries kept her in that calming place for the rest of the day.

"Go play," I urged her. "This field is yours. We are watching and will protect you. Roll in the grass, play in the water, and chase your own butterfly."

"No thanks," she seemed to say (again, we didn't converse), "I'm right where I want to be."

I was so frustrated I wanted to choke her. From her comfortable spot, she watched Rhett jump, gallop, roll, and chase butterflies in every bend and crook of that meadow. Ashley did not move so the fence was actually built *around* her. Dusk approached and it took four of us to catch Rhett and force him behind the gate where Ashley calmly sat. Once inside, though, Rhett dropped in utter exhaustion. After all, joyously discovering a whole new world is hard work! He blissfully experienced a world Ashley would never know simply because she was only content in her familiar world behind the gate.

Stupid dog!

Alarmingly, though, I recognized the Ashley in me. How many times have I missed a blessing because I didn't want to leave the comfort of where I was? How many boundaries have I created that kept me from enjoying all the world had to offer? How often should I have been forging a new road when I actually preferred to ignore the challenges facing me? How many times have I watched the action around me when, all along, God was calling me to get involved?

Move. Get up. Explore and take a chance, recognizing that your true security is found in God. There will be difficult days,

> **How often should I have been forging a new road when I actually preferred to ignore the challenges facing me?**

to be sure. But there will also be days you find yourself playing in refreshing streams and chasing beautiful butterflies. The world waits. But first you have to open the gate.

Cathy Lee Phillips

LETTERS TO GOD FROM DOGS

Dear God, How come people love to smell flowers, but seldom, if ever, smell one another? Where are their priorities?

Dear God, When we get to Heaven, can we sit on your couch? Or is it the same old story?

Dear God, Excuse me, but why are there cars named after the jaguar, the cougar, the mustang, the colt, the stingray, and the rabbit, but not one named for a dog? How often do you see a cougar riding around? We dogs love a nice ride! I know every breed cannot have its own model, but it would be easy to rename the Chrysler Eagle the Chrysler Beagle!

Dear God, Is it true that in Heaven, dining room tables have on-ramps?

Dear God, When we get to the Pearly Gates, do we have to shake hands to get in?

Dear God, Are there dogs on other planets, or are we alone? I have been howling at the moon and stars for a long time, but all I ever hear back is the beagle across the street!

Dear God, Are there mailmen in Heaven? If there are, will I have to apologize?

Dear God, When my family eats dinner they always bless their food. But they never bless mine. So I've been wagging my tail extra fast when they fill my bowl. Have you noticed my own blessing?

Dear God, I've always lived at the shelter and I have everything I need. But many of the cats here have names and I don't. Could you give me a name please? It would be good for my self-esteem.

Dear God, The new terrier I live with just peed on the Oriental rug and I have a feeling my family might blame me 'cuz they think I'm jealous of this stupid dog. Since they have no sense of smell, how can I convince them I'm innocent? Does Petsmart sell lie detectors?

Mark Bricklin

• •

Did you hear that NASA has launched several Holsteins into low earth orbit?

It was the herd shot around the world.

Prairie Home Companion

• •

I don't think you can trust him, Fifi. If you ask me, I think he's a wolf.

CHACA, UH UH . . .

The phone rang and my first thoughts were, "Who died?" Why else would anybody call at 12:20 A.M. other than to tell you somebody had died?

"Hello," I answered. This better be really good or really bad, I thought.

"Richmond, how would you like a little adventure in your life?" I recognized the voice of my boss, the zoo's young but very capable veterinarian.

"Sure, what's up?"

"The police just called. They want us to catch a killer ape that's loose in Highland Park. Meet me at the zoo in a few minutes."

As I hung up the phone I found myself wishing he had not said "killer ape." Of course if a killer ape were loose in Highland Park it would need our help. That was a rough neighborhood.

I pushed my car to its limits and the freeway lights and signs charged me like an onslaught of wooden soldiers. They briefly appeared in my rear-view mirror and quickly faded from view. As I drove, I made an an inventory of what we might need in the capture of a killer ape. Tranquilizer gun, nets, ropes, and assorted drugs. My damp palms gripped the steering wheel, and I wondered if my boss would notice if I didn't show up. I was probably the only one he called, so I concluded he might.

I skidded around the freeway off-ramp and entered the zoo's immense parking lot. Waiting at the entrance to the zoo was a black-and-white police car, its red and yellow lights pulsating with anticipation. Two officers were sitting in the front seat.

"Your boss is already at the health center. He wanted us to bring you up." I jumped in the back of the police car and we screamed past the security guard who was manning the gate. "Killer ape, huh?" I asked.

"Tore up his master real good. Went after one of our officers too. That ape is one mean son of a gun." (The officer didn't exactly say "son of a gun.") "One of our guys discharged his revolver at it, but he missed. We'll get the sucker, though."

By the time we pulled up to the zoo health center, Dr. Bill Hulsizer had already gathered everything we would need. We threw it in the trunk and jumped into the back seat. The car lurched forward, and in no time we were on the freeway with the siren howling. We passed several cars, all of which looked as though they were standing still. I glanced at the speedometer and noticed that we were going ninety miles an hour.

I turned toward Bill and asked, "So what do you think we're up against?"

He was the scientific type and would not speculate. He shrugged his shoulders and said, "We'll see."

I have always suffered from an over-active imagination, and it wouldn't have surprised me if King Kong himself stepped on the police car when we got there. We flew down the off-ramp and wove our way deep into a residential area. It looked as though we had entered a war zone. The officers were stopped by a crusty sergeant who pointed into the night and said, "They're waitin' for you at the command post."

"Command post," I said with a tinge of sarcasm in my voice. "What did you get us into, Doctor?"

"We'll see," he said with a wry smile. Boy, sometimes those scientific types can really make you mad.

There were police cars everywhere. All of them had their lights flashing on and off, and all of the neighbors were clustered in small groups, discussing the crisis. We arrived at the command post, and an officer with plenty of authority called for a mass meeting. Officers began showing up from everywhere. I'm sure there were more than fifty. We were brought to the center of the group and the officer with all the authority said, "Men, this is Dr. Bill Hulsizer and his assistant Gary Richmond. These guys are experts from the zoo. They're going to help us track down the ape." He turned to us and said, "You guys are in charge. What do you want us to do?"

Bill and I looked at each other and I think we both wanted to laugh. Bill was the shy type. He was a very competent veterinarian, but there was no way he was going to order around the policemen that surrounded us. I didn't want to usurp his authority so I waited for him to make the first move. He put his arm on my shoulder and said, "Gary is the capture expert. Let's let him take charge."

"Take it," said the man with the biggest badge. So I did.

"Is there anybody here who has actually seen the animal we are after?" I probed.

A young officer stepped forward and said, "I did, sir."

"Can you describe him for us?"

"The light wasn't too hot. He was big, though. I discharged my revolver at him, but I believe I missed. Scared the heck out of me." (The officer didn't exactly say "heck.")

"Is the owner around here or any neighbors who have seen the animal? It would really be helpful if we knew what we were after."

The owner's father was brought to us, and as it turned out, he was the man who had been attacked. Most of his upper body was bandaged, including his face. The owner was in jail on several counts, all having to do with possessing or selling narcotics. It seems that he had developed a drug habit in Vietnam and brought it home with him. That's not all he brought with him. He also brought home a young pet that grew up to be something very large and very dangerous. I asked the man if he had a photograph of his son's pet. He said he did and reached for his wallet. As he handed me the picture he explained how he had sustained his injuries. It seems that while his son was in jail the responsibility of feeding the creature was his. The creature only liked the son, and

He also brought home a young pet that grew up to be something very large and very dangerous.

attempting to get food into the cage was a daily act of courage. This was the night the father lost the battle. Blood was seeping through his gauze bandages, and I could just feel the tension building among the officers. I studied the photograph and was somewhat relieved to discover that the "killer ape" was really just a large monkey. It was a stump-tailed macaque—a very large specimen with two-inch canines.

I addressed the father once more, "Is there anything the monkey likes?" I was thinking of a favorite food item and was unprepared for the man's answer.

He was a Mexican-American gentleman and said with great enthusiasm, "Chaca likes it when you say, 'Chaca, Uh Uh.' I don't know why, but it calms him down." I thanked him very much for his help and began to speak to the assembly of policemen.

"Officers, I have very good news for you. We are not after a killer ape but a very large monkey named Chaca. Chaca is not the kind of animal that you would need to shoot, and frankly, I will not help you look for him if *I* have to worry about getting shot. If it would make you feel better, carry your night sticks. The owner's father has just told me that their pet likes it when you say, 'Chaca, Uh Uh,' so I suggest that as you go through the neighborhood you repeat that phrase over and over. We will wait here until he is sighted then we will take over. He is most likely scared to death after being shot at and is simply hiding."

As the officers spread out, Dr. Hulsizer leaned over to me and said, "Gary, it's not going to do any good for them to be saying, 'Chaca, Uh Uh.'"

"It will too. It will keep them calm. If they think they're helping their own cause they might not shoot each other." Then Bill and I got the giggles as Los Angeles's finest went from house to house and from garage to garage saying, "Chaca, Uh Uh."

A police helicopter thundered overhead and turned on its

blinding searchlight. Backyards were bathed in light, and although it was 2:00 A.M. we had the passing sensation of walking about in broad daylight. Walkie-talkies crackled and squeaked as policemen checked in to report that they had not sighted Chaca. The helicopter search was finally called off, and we again heard the masculine chant, "Chaca, Uh Uh . . . Chaca, Uh Uh." It sounded like a soundtrack from an old jungle movie and it would have fit the moment if someone had said, "The natives are getting restless."

At 2:45 A.M., an officer came running up to us and announced that his partner had Chaca cornered in a garage. We grabbed our equipment and hurried to the site. Most of the policemen were already there. They parted to let us through so that we might enter the side door of the garage. When we got inside, we saw Chaca huddled under a small fishing boat which was sitting snugly on its boat trailer. Chaca was protecting his face from the bright beam of light that issued forth from the sergeant's blue-steel flashlight. Chaca's body language was screaming, "Don't shoot, please don't shoot!"

His capture was not in the least dramatic. We laid a net over his trembling body and he fell over. I believe he was very near to fainting. We transferred Chaca to a travel cage and took him back to the zoo. He was kept there for thirty days in quarantine to determine whether or not he was carrying any transmissible diseases. He was then moved to another facility and we never saw him again.

It was after 4:00 A.M. when I crawled back into bed. It had been a great adventure and one with a happy, injury-free conclusion. It was clearly one of the most memorable experiences of my entire life. I cannot recall any deliberate thought concerning God during the whole night. But He was there, caring, protecting. And I can't prove it but I think He was laughing.

Gary Richmond

●●●

A house without a pet is lonely, quiet, calm, and . . . clean.

How utterly boring!

Mary Hollingsworth

●●●

7

Hamsters, Toads, Fish, and Snakes—What Odd Companions We Take!

Now, personally, I think people who love snakes are a little off their crock. Still, snakes are intriguing. And what fun it is to watch a little boy with his first frog. God has added such humor to life through his unique creations.

FOUR-LEGGED FRIEND

Horses have always been part of my life. For years my husband, Conrad, and I owned horses and boarded others on our farm in Minnesota. It wasn't easy work, but I loved my animals. One horse stood out over all the others: Schatze. The nickname means "sweetheart," because that's what he was from the very start. I should know; I owned his mother, and I was there when he was foaled, 23 years ago. He grew into a beauty, two white socks on his hind legs, a star between his soulful eyes. Schatze was my pride and joy.

With our three children grown and off on their own, life on the farm became harder. One morning after cleaning the horse stalls, my body ached so badly that I wanted to crawl back into bed.

"I can't do this anymore," I told Conrad.

He surprised me. "I can't either," he said.

Conrad was from Texas, and he'd always wanted to go back. We were almost sixty. Maybe it was time to make the move. The kids didn't want us to leave, but Conrad and I bought a small house near Austin. Simple. Low maintenance. Just what we were after. We sold the farm. It was painful, especially to sell horses I loved, but we quickly found good homes for all of them. Except one.

Schatze was slightly lame for no apparent reason. We couldn't sell him as a sound horse. I'd never wanted to give him up, not ever, but there'd be no place for him in the city. I had to find the right home. Just before our moving deadline, the sister of an acquaintance asked to have Schatze to trail ride.

"He'd live on a Wisconsin farm," she said. "with a pony and a few calves." It sounded so nice. Schatze would be happy, and that's what mattered. I told her how to care for him, how he liked to give kisses for carrots or apples.

"Just love him," I finally said. I gave him to her in return for that promise from her. No charge. It was too much. I wrapped my arms around Schatze's neck and sobbed. Ten years together. Leaving him was the hardest thing I'd ever done.

We'd been wrong to think we could go from one extreme to the other. Whenever I talked to family in Minnesota, I dissolved into grief. Conrad wasn't doing much better in our cramped surroundings. Our yard was a postage stamp full of sand burrs. I'd once worked happily, sunup to sundown. Now

I had little to do except sit at the computer, and I only felt worse physically. I began to hurt everywhere. So much for city life.

Eventually we found a 40-acre ranch with a few cows. It was nowhere near the work we'd left behind in Minnesota. Just enough. And this time, it was the right move. We were back in the country, with enough room to breathe. If only we had Schatze.

One morning I noticed a piece of paper on the floor. *I'll pick it up later*, I thought. That wasn't like me. After a while I couldn't tie my shoelaces or get out of a chair. Conrad had to help me put on my socks. Making a bed was a Herculean effort. Climbing stairs was torture.

> **The diagnosis was polymyalgia, a type of arthritis that affects the muscles.**

"I feel like I'm a hundred years old," I told Conrad.

He insisted I see a doctor. The diagnosis was polymyalgia, a type of arthritis that affects the muscles. The doctor gave me a corticosteroid drug, and I felt better until I learned that a possible side effect was osteoporosis. That worried me. Strong pain medications only made me sick. Finally I just stuck to aspirin, and prayed for relief. Was this what getting older felt like?

I got into bed one night, my whole body tight as a drum. I ached from head to toe, in places I didn't even know I had muscles. *Lord, give me something to focus on besides my pain.* I wanted to like my life again. I wanted to be me. I often thought of Schatze, remembering his sweetness, hoping he was okay.

Conrad decided a trip back home to Minnesota would do me good. A letter arrived just before we left, from a girl who had worked on our farm. She sent a picture of a horse. He looked unkempt and thin. But that star! Those eyes! The two white hind socks! It was Schatze. He was at the university vet school, donated to be used as a blood donor. Not a good life.

I visited the university soon after we arrived in Minnesota. There he was.

"Schatze," I whispered, "I'm so sorry."

He nuzzled my cheek. Tears filled my eyes. He was still my precious horse, but different now. Lethargic, sad.

"We have to do something," I begged Conrad. But what? How could this have happened to him?

I had a restless night. Sometime in the middle of my tossing and turning, I heard something. A voice: "What is the desire of your heart?"

I looked over at Conrad. He was sound asleep. "Who's there?" I whispered.

Again, that question. I wasn't dreaming. But how to explain what I was hearing? *The desire of my heart?* It was so simple. But saying it couldn't make it so.

"The desire of my heart is to have my horse again." The idea was impossible. But there it was. A Bible promise came to mind, Psalm 37: "Have your delight in the Lord and He will give you the desires of your heart." I hardly dared believe it.

The next morning Conrad and I had a long talk. We determined to get Schatze back, but we couldn't obtain his release from the university. We returned to Texas without him. One image stayed constant in my mind: my beloved horse.

We waited months and months, advised by the university that only when they were "through with him," could we buy him. The pain I lived with grew worse, but I decided to put my faith to work. I needed to do something concrete to show God that I really believed in him.

I got to work. I wanted to be sure Schatze would be safe around the barbed wire fence on our ranch. I twisted white plastic ties on every wire to make the fence more visible. Finally the university released Schatze. Our children pooled their money and bought him for us. That was one of the happiest days of my life. Now, how to get him home?

A former neighbor called. She had a horse trailer. She'd bring him down to Texas!

Schatze needed me full time when he came back. I couldn't retreat to my bed. I had to feed him, groom him, care for his feet—all the things you must do to keep a horse happy and healthy. He came back to me very head shy. I had to regain his trust, attending to him as if he were a foal again. He had to learn that no one would mistreat him. He was my focus. I all but forgot about my pain.

Then the day arrived when he lowered his head into my arms. "Schatze," I told him, "you're home."

He became himself again, and I'm as much me as I ever was. I needed him as much as he needed me. I'm still a bit creaky in the hinges, but at sixty-eight, that's not bad. Schatze and I can grow old together. I love him, the desire of my heart.

Gail J. Huffstutler

••

I found a snake in my yard and got a shovel and whacked the fire out of it. Then I didn't have cable for a week.

Charlie Viracola

••

THE GARBAGE DISPOSAL

My mother's first car was a little white Corvair that my father bought for her. She dearly loved that car and, when they later sold it, missed it. Around the same time frame, back in the early 1960s, she was also gifted with a garbage disposal. This apparently was a big deal back at that time since these were new items for the home; therefore not many people had one yet. As any sibling would do in my mother's shoes, she called up one of her sisters to brag about the new disposal.

"Oh boy," my Aunt W sighed wistfully after hearing my mother share about Dad surprising her with a garbage disposal.

"I know," my mother replied. "At first I didn't think I would like it. Now I am spoiled by the silly thing, W."

That sounds so nice! I wish we could get one but . . ." W sighed wistfully again.

"I know where I can get you one!"

"You do?" W asked my mother excitedly.

"Oh sure," Mom replied with a smile while playing with the phone cord. "I tell you what; I'll pick it up and drive it down to you this week-end. Just think of it as a late birthday gift or something."

"Really? That will be great," W was on Cloud 9 hearing of my mother's grand plan.

"Well, isn't that what sisters are for?" Mom smiled.

My sister, a few days later in the driveway, was far from Cloud 9. "You just do these things to embarrass me," she pouted.

Interstate 70 didn't exist yet, so my mother had to drive up U.S. 40 through downtown Indianapolis to get on another highway that would take them to her hometown in southern Indiana. Of course, this also meant driving down the "main streets" of various small towns along the way.

At every stoplight, my sister slouched down further in the front passenger seat. Each time my mother brought the car to a stop or stepped on the gas again, the garbage disposal would rock back and forth in the trunk . . . that, in a Corvair, was placed in front and the engine was in back of the car. Each time the garbage disposal rocked, it naturally made noise. My sister would slink down as far as she could in the car seat. My mother ignored my sister and looked straight ahead during the two-hour drive.

When Mom pulled the Corvair into Aunt W's driveway,

my sister jumped out and made her escape as soon as the car came to a halt. She brushed past Aunt W, who was coming out to greet them. No doubt my sister was rushing to hide in one of her cousin's bedrooms seeking comfort and understanding about how a teenager feels about having "unusual" parents to deal with.

"How was your trip?" W asked while bounding down the side steps of her house.

"Not bad at all," Mom replied while walking to the front of the car. "Traffic was fairly light. Ready to see your new disposal?"

"Oh boy, am I," Aunt W smiled broadly as she joined Mom in front of the car. "Is it very heavy?" she asked.

"Well," my mother said while putting the key in the lock, "Bob and I both had to lift it into the trunk, so I figure it will take both of us to get it out. But we will have to be quick," she added cryptically while starting to lift the lid of the trunk . . . not giving my aunt a chance to ask what she meant about having to be quick.

Aunt W screamed and jumped back as a pig poked its head up, grunting and snorting at the women as a way of sharing verbal displeasure about its trip. Then before either of them could react, the animal clambered out of the trunk and took off running across the backyard. My aunt looked at my mother and muttered something as they both took off in high-heeled pursuit of the squealing animal.

"I'll get you for this," Marge," W hollered. "Garbage disposal. Ha. Ha. Ha."

They did not manage to catch the pig. Every once in a while my Aunt W would share with us about someone claiming to have seen a pig running around town loose. We cannot be for certain if it was Aunt W's "garbage disposal" or just another pig that happened to be roaming around town.

Carol Wells

••

The truth is, a snake might never hurt me. But it can surely make me hurt myself as I'm trying to get away from it.

Mary Hollingsworth

••

ELEPHANT AND TURTLE

An elephant was drinking out of a river one day, when he spotted a turtle asleep on a log. So, he ambled on over and kicked it clear across the river.

"What did you do that for?" asked a passing giraffe.

"Because I recognized it as the same turtle that took a nip out of my trunk 53 years ago."

"Wow, what a memory," commented the giraffe.

"Yes," said the elephant, "turtle recall."

Author Unknown

••

A myth is a moth's sister.

Stan Laurel

••

FISH STORIES

Row, row, row your boat,
Catch a fish today.
And keep your story straight about
The one that got away.

A FISH STORY

Father-son (or father-daughter) fishing trips are a great way to develop family closeness. Catching the fish, frying it up, and eating it together—it doesn't get any better than that.

Now, any fisherman worth his salt can tell you stories about "the one that got away—that Moby-esque catch of a lifetime that was very nearly snagged using only one anemic worm and extraordinary fishing skills.

My husband, an avid fisherman, has more fish tales than Mrs. Paul. He's caught bass, catfish, shark, seaweed, and enough empty soda cans to make our house payment for three months. He even taught each of our sons to fish. I have never quite mastered the sport myself. I don't come back with stories about the *fish* that got away. I return with stories about the *fishing pole* that got away.

That's why I usually let father and son go on their outings alone. They bring back the fish and I burn it. It just works better that way. There was that one time, though, when my husband got a little *too* excited over one of their catches.

"Now, *this* beauty deserves to be mounted," he said proudly, holding up the fish.

"That's lovely, dear," I commented, underwhelmed. "But hardly worth mounting. How about a nice key chain instead?"

"Are you kidding? This baby needs to be where everyone can see it!" he said, beaming. "You know, like professional fishermen do."

"You're not really going to call a taxidermist for *that*, are you?" I asked.

He shook his head. "I'm not trusting this prize catch to a taxidermist. Besides, who knows what they'd charge? I'll do it myself."

And with that, he headed for the garage.

Recalling the garbage disposal he repaired himself (at four

> Gutting it,
> though, made
> that poor critter
> lose what little
> fullness it had.

times the cost of a professional plumber) and the washing machine he helped to run more quietly (after he worked on it, it never ran again), I decided I'd better follow.

"Have you ever done anything like this before?" I asked as he laid the fish on his work table.

"No," he shrugged. "But how hard could it be?"

The first step was to gut the fish. That seemed logical enough. Gutting it, though, made that poor critter lose what little fullness it had. It now appeared almost two-dimensional, so he decided to plump it up with pieces of newspaper.

After the fish had all the news he could stomach (I know the feeling), he was ready to be preserved. My husband mounted him onto a board using various brackets and hooks. Then, taking a can of resin from the shelf, he proceeded to baste that poor fish into posterity. Five coats of resin later that fish was destined to be with us forever.

Unfortunately, so was the smell.

With each passing day, we became more and more aware of the fact that resin doesn't lock in odor. For three years our house had the lovely aroma of a fish cannery. Summers were the worst. Those 104-degree days do wonders for aged trout.

After one particularly grueling heat wave, I managed to talk my husband into taking a final picture (Kodak memories don't smell) before tossing out the shriveled-up souvenir. After all, it was the humane thing to do for the poor fish . . . and for everyone within a three-mile radius of our house. Besides, the fish had begun to look like an elongated prune with eyes.

But that was all right. Both my husband and my son knew there were plenty of other fish in the sea. And even though that pungent souvenir of their fishing trip was finally gone, the memory of their time together was sure to last forever.

Martha Bolton

Dog Property Laws

If I like it, it's mine.

If it's in my mouth, it's mine.

If I can take it from you, it's mine.

If I had it a little while ago, it's mine.

If it's mine, it must never appear to be yours in any way.

If I'm chewing something up, all the pieces are mine.

If it just looks like mine, it's mine.

If I saw it first, it's mine.

If you are playing with something and you put it down, it automatically becomes mine.

If it's broken, it's yours.

F. L. Saucy

When the mouse laughs at the cat there's a hole nearby.

Nigerian Proverb

GOING NUTS OVER SQUIRRELS

My dog Catfish, the black Labrador, has been trying unsuccessfully for some time to catch a squirrel in the backyard, and I am concerned this failure eventually will lead him to a nervous breakdown, or even worse.

I have a great number of trees in my backyard, and count-less squirrels cavort among them. When Catfish is outside and spots a squirrel, he immediately dashes after it.

I think the squirrels have taken to tantalizing him. They allow Catfish to get just beyond striking distance, and then they dash away and up a tree and look down at my frustrated dog and laugh at him.

Catfish returns from squirrel chasings with a pained, dis-appointed look on his face. I think he has become obsessed with catching at least one squirrel.

I've tried to trick him into thinking he has caught one. I bought a stuffed squirrel and put it in the yard. Catfish spot-ted it and attacked. When it didn't run away, he became sus-picious. He wasn't dealing with a bona fide squirrel here, and brought it into the house and laid it at my feet, as if to say, "Nice try, Dad, but if it's not the real thing, I'm not interested."

Even if the frustration of coming up empty time and again doesn't make Catfish loony, there is also the problem of what happens when my dog is inside my house and sees a squirrel on the outside.

The back of my house is a series of glass doors, which remain closed most of the time. Catfish has not figured out the theory of glass. He sees a squirrel outside and goes dash-ing for it and runs into the glass at approximately 65 mph.

"You can't run through glass," I tell him after he has regained consciousness. He gives me that pained, disappointed look again, along with his flattened nose and crossed eyes.

I'm torn here, as one might imagine. I want my dog to live a happy, healthy life and not become brain-damaged. Perhaps, I have thought, if he were to catch just one lousy squirrel, he would be free of this obsession.

On the other hand, I don't want any harm to come to any of the squirrels who live in my backyard. They're cute little boogers, and I enjoy watching them run around in the grass and straw looking for whatever it is squirrels look for.

This experience—and dilemma—has taught me to have a great deal of appreciation for the order of nature.

Dogs naturally chase squirrels, but squirrels are naturally faster than dogs. They scamper up trees to get away from dogs, who have no earthly idea how to climb a tree.

Glass doors, on the other hand, are not a part of the natural order of things.

I simply hope that if one day Catfish crashes headfirst into another one in hot pursuit of a squirrel and suffers a fatal injury, he will somehow know it was the door, not the squirrel, his avowed enemy, who killed him.

Lewis Grizzard

Polka Dots, Stripes, Humps and Hatracks

I've always been fascinated with animals. And it occurs to me that God could have simply made all animals round and gray, if he had wanted to. But he didn't. Instead, the great Artist of the universe had a blast creating the wonderful menagerie we call the Animal Kingdom, and he must have laughed with joy as he did it. Think about it—he created . . .

Polka dotted leopards and Dalmatians.

Zebras and tigers with racing stripes.

Raccoons with ring-around-the-tail and a pair of glasses.

An octopus with eight squirmy legs and a great big head.

Curious cats with long fur, short fur, white, black, brown, and gray fur. Then, just for fun, he splashed one with calico!

Dogs with their own fur coats.

One-hump and two-hump camels.

Birds with funny feathered hats.

Giraffes with stretched-out necks.

Bucktoothed beavers with wide, flat tails.

A kangaroo with a built-in purse.

A firefly with a light for seeing in the dark.

Scary, hairy spiders with ugly, fuzzy legs.

Funny noses on elephants and anteaters.

Long, floppy ears and short, perky ears.

Curly, twirly tails on pigs and o'possums.

Big, flat feet on bunnies and elephants. Funny, webbed feet on ducks and platypuses. Lots of feet on centipedes. And no feet on snakes.

Flying bats with built-in radar.

Skunks with strange perfume.

Hooked-nose parrots that whistle and talk.

And that's just for starters!

And the Bible says, then "God looked at everything He had made, and it was very good." (Genesis 1:31 ICB)

Mary Hollingsworth

A BOY'S FIRST FROG

My grandson stood in the open garage door looking out at the summer rain that had spoiled his plans to stretch the day by playing outside in the dark and maybe even chasing fireflies.

Just as he was about to go inside, he saw it—a jumping rock. Then he realized it was not a rock at all, but something better—a FROG—the stuff a young boy's dreams are made of. It's raining frogs, he thought; maybe it really does rain frogs!

He ran inside wide-eyed to tell the news, "I saw a frog!"

"Are you sure?"

"Yes, it's a frog, come and see."

And sure enough the frog was still there hunched down on the wet driveway in the rain. "Can we catch it?" he asked. How could anyone refuse the request of a wide-eyed boy who wanted to chase a frog?

The frog sensed trouble and went hopping down the driveway with my grandson hopping behind him squealing with delight, and my daughter skipping puddles in the rain. After several attempts, the elusive frog was captured.

The child held it in his small hands, feeling the life in the creature.

"Can I take it inside?"

The frog was placed in a bucket that was too deep for the creature to jump out, and taken inside to the light of the kitchen to admire. My grandson looked at its bulging frog eyes, its webbed feet, and touched its amphibian skin with wonder. It was a fine frog.

A boy's first frog is a big event in life. Grandma brought the camera out to record the occasion as the boy beamed with excitement and posed with the captured wild life.

"Can I keep it?" he pleaded.

"You can keep it for a little while, but then you have to turn it loose so it can go home."

"But why?"

Grasping for a reason that a five-year-old could comprehend without being told the gruesome details of a wild creature's slow death in captivity, my daughter replied, "Its mother will be worried."

My grandson looked thoughtful, then suggested, "Maybe we could catch the mother too?"

A child's simple logic demands truth.

"Wild creatures need to be free, even frogs," explained his mother. "Wild things cannot live unless they are free."

Finally, he understood and nodded. "Well, I'll just keep it for a little while," he said, still not ready to give up ownership of such a fascinating bug-eyed creature.

Too soon it was time to return the frog to its environment. The bucket was taken outside and turned on its side, and the creature hopped away and disappeared into the flowerbed.

My grandson tried to find it among the daylilies the next morning, but the frog was gone back to wherever frogs go to hide when there is no torrential rain in which to play.

My grandson is still young. There will be more rain in his life and other frogs that will come out on dark nights from secret places. But this frog will always be special—there will never be another frog exactly like this one.

It was a boy's first frog.

Sheila Moss

....

Last year for my birthday I was given a puppy. It's half poodle, and half pit bull. Not a good attack dog, but a vicious gossip.

Bob Smith

....

"Cleveland, Ohio? We have fins,
so I always assumed we lived in Finland!"

8

Tricks and Treats

A lot of the fun and frolicking that we love about our pets comes from the tricks they do. With the right delectable treats, they'll do everything from playing dead to the Texas Two-Step.

CRACKERJACK

One of the most interesting pets I ever owned was a conure parrot named Crackerjack. He was beautiful with bright green feathers, a brilliant orange comb, and a sunny yellow chest and underwings. He had snapping black eyes and loved to talk in his gravely voice. When you said, "What's your name?" he replied, "Crackerjack! Crackerjack! I'm a crackerjack!" He was a character.

Crackerjack lived in a huge cage by the window overlooking Black Bayou, which encircled Treasure Island—the housing edition in Monroe, Louisiana, where our house was located. He squawked at the passersby and jabbered from dawn till dusk at anything and everything.

My husband, Lestle, had a unique relationship with

Crackerjack. When he came home from the office and pulled into the garage, Crackerjack recognized his car engine and immediately began squawking. Lestle responded from the garage with a similar sound. And they chatted back and forth until my husband got into the house and over to Crackerjack's cage to scratch his head. Only then would the bird stop squawking.

Then Lestle would put his cheek next to the cage and say, "Give us a kiss." And Crackerjack would tease him by running across to the other side of the cage, bobbing his head up and down, and saying over and over, "Give us a kiss, sweetie. Give us a kiss, sweetie."

Finally, though, he would inch his way over to Lestle coyly and gently nibble Lestle's check with his bill, saying softly, "Give us a kiss, sweetie." And Lestle would then scratch Crackerjack's head again. It was a ritual they both enjoyed.

One day I was sitting in the den where Crackerjack's cage was, watching him play and laughing at his antics. He would stand on one perch and then reach out as far as his neck would stretch and grab onto another perch with his bill and swing himself up and over onto the second perch. He did this over and over, just for fun. As I was watching, he stretched out his neck to repeat the act, but he missed the second perch, which threw him off balance. And suddenly he was hanging upside down by his feet from the first perch. I fell out laughing as he said rather quietly, "Uh oh."

My favorite incident happened one evening when we had dinner guests at the house. Crackerjack was jabbering in his normal, happy manner. These folks had not been to our house before, so they were unfamiliar with Crackerjack's wide vocabulary and actions. We were enjoying our dessert when I heard a siren in the distance, and I thought, *Hmmmm. This should be interesting.*

As the siren came closer and closer, suddenly Crackerjack started his favorite routine. In his cage were a number of parrot toys, which parrots—known as the "clown bird"—love, including a variety of perches, a mirror, a ladder, and a bell.

He began to run back and forth in his cage, screaming, "Help! Help!" Then he would swing wildly from perch to perch to perch, squawking and screaming. "Here it comes! Here it comes!" And he would bob his head up and down, up and down, while making a crying sound and moaning, "Oh no, oh no, oh no."

By this time our guests were looking around to see what this crazy bird was doing. Knowing what was coming next, Lestle and I were struggling to keep straight faces.

Finally, as the siren went screaming past our house on its way to somewhere else, Crackerjack ran up and down his ladder yelling, "Fire! Fire!" and ringing his bell over and over. "Fire! Fire!" Ding, ding, ding!

By this time our guests were cracking up, we were dying with laughter, and Crackerjack was exhausted. Lestle rewarded him with some bites of banana, his favorite treat, and we returned to our dessert.

"How in the world did you ever teach him to do all that?" asked one of our guests.

"We didn't," I replied solemnly. "He really thinks he's a fireman."

I miss that wonderful bird. He was a good friend.

Mary Hollingsworth

SHADOW AND THE BISCUITS

When I finished breakfast that Saturday morning, I faced a dilemma. What is the proper means of disposing of two crispy biscuits? I decided that instead of placing them in the garbage, I would give them to Shadow.

Shadow is the newest addition to the Phillips household.

He is a golden retriever mix adopted from the local animal shelter. My previous dog, Victory, passed away last year on Christmas Eve. Victory was a special dog and it was very hard to lose my faithful canine companion, especially on Christmas Eve.

Though I waited several months, I quickly realized that I wanted another dog.

"What kind of dog do you want?" people asked.

"I don't know," I responded. "But I will know him when I see him."

One warm day, my friend, Caroline Sosebee, and her two sons, Brandon and Trace, decided it was time for me to find a new dog. We piled into Caroline's new just-off-the-lot van and invaded the local animal shelter. After examining all sorts of dogs, my eyes landed on the creature I knew was destined to be my dog. He was happy, cute, and friendly—everything I wanted. The only problem was the wicked woman who saw him first and threw her body between the dog and me.

Not wanting me to start a brawl at the local animal shelter, Caroline suggested that I find another dog.

"No," I insisted. "This is my dog."

I watched helplessly as this wicked woman took my dog outside to *bond* with him before finalizing the adoption. Was it horrible of me to pray the dog would bite her? No serious injury, of course. A tiny nick with a small loss of blood would be sufficient.

Moments later, the woman brought my dog back into the kennel. Knowing that I had the dog in my sights, she said to me, "He is a fence climber and I will just not have that."

I was delighted! I have a six-foot wooden fence. And I was thankful that the dog was going to be mine without the animal actually having to bite the woman.

The Sosebee clan and I took the dog outside to an enclosed "bonding area." Brandon and I played with and petted the dog. Trace, afraid of the abundance of canine energy, curled up in Caroline's lap and gave his approval of the dog from a distance. While I was bonding with the dog, so was Brandon. For a moment I thought I might actually have to adopt both Brandon and the dog because they were quickly becoming a matched set. In fact, Brandon volunteered to sit with the dog while I completed paperwork and wrote a check that made him the official dog of the Phillips household. In a matter of minutes we had placed the golden puppy on a blanket in the back of Caroline's van and were happily on our way home.

I was so thankful Caroline had volunteered her van in which to transport the dog. It was far roomier than my car. And, I'll admit, I was especially thankful to be in Caroline's van when the dog experienced a case of motion sickness and "baptized" the vehicle. Even though we stopped and cleaned everything, that "new car" smell certainly disappeared that day.

Driving quite a bit slower, we crept home without further incident. I placed the dog in the fence where Brandon continued to play happily with him. In view of their special connection, I conferred upon Brandon the title of the *Doggie Godfather*. He was thrilled—Brandon, that is. I don't think the dog noticed.

Within a few minutes we named the dog Shadow because he shadowed me wherever I went. He stayed right with me and was obviously quite content with his new home. He's been a happy puppy since that day.

But, back to the biscuits.

Shadow is always happy to see me. He is even happier when I come bearing food. I held out the first biscuit and Shadow sniffed it then quickly seized it from my hand. Of course, I also love this dog because he is nonjudgmental and did not care that the biscuit was a tad burned (well, crispy!).

I waited for Shadow to gobble the biscuit but was interested when he marched around the yard while holding the

> **Within a few minutes we named the dog Shadow because he shadowed me wherever I went.**

biscuit tightly in his mouth. Intrigued (and almost insulted), I realized he was going to hide his biscuit. I supposed it would be a great mid-afternoon snack when his daily serving of Wal-Mart Old Roy Dog Food had been digested. Shadow marched from one end of the yard to the other, surveying, sniffing, and finally locating a spot to conceal his biscuit. On the right side of the yard, next to the fence, Shadow began to dig a hole.

He dug with his front paws and burrowed with his nose, never letting the biscuit leave his mouth. But he suddenly stopped, obviously not satisfied with the location.

Becoming quite impatient I spoke to Shadow in a stern voice, "Go ahead! Eat the biscuit. I have another one waiting for you in the kitchen."

The dog ignored me and, again, marched around the yard. He started and stopped his digging several more times, causing me further irritation.

"Eat the biscuit, you crazy dog. Eat it and I will let you have the other biscuit, too. Doggone it!"

Again, the dog ignored me. I went back inside, finished cleaning the kitchen, and about an hour later presented Shadow with the second crispy biscuit, which he eagerly accepted.

So what did I learn on an ordinary Saturday morning from one hairy dog and two crispy biscuits? Like me, Shadow had a problem letting go. He held on to what he had, not realizing that by giving up the first biscuit, he could have a second one.

How often I have been content with one small crispy biscuit when God wanted to bless me with so much more. All that I needed was simply to let go of what I thought was my security and instead, truly trust God to take care of me.

Shadow enjoyed two crispy biscuits that Saturday morning because he finally found the courage to let go of the first biscuit.

Lord, help me to embrace the blessing you have in store for

me. When the time is right, grant me the courage to let go of the "comfortable" and trust You to guide me to the "wonderful!"

Cathy Lee Phillips

• •

A man followed a woman and her dog out of a movie theater. He stopped her and said, "I'm sorry to bother you, but I couldn't help noticing that your dog was really into the movie. He cried at the right spots and fidgeted in his seat at the boring parts. Most of all, he laughed like crazy at the funny parts. Did you find that unusual?"

"Yes," she replied, "because he hated the book!"

Jim Kraus

• •

**"I've got 273 fleas who haven't paid their rent.
Let me talk to Judge Judy!"**

MEET WALTER

I took my dog to the vet this morning.

Walter is a white German shepherd puppy, although I used the word *puppy* loosely. This is because Walter slobbers like a fire hydrant. He eats like a vacuum. And when he's not trying to scramble onto my lap like a fifty-pound Pomeranian, he's ricocheting around the house like a loose balloon on amphetamines.

So you can see why, when Walter started moping around the house a few days ago, I knew something was wrong.

I got the prognosis (and the bill) this morning.

Walter has tonsillitis.

I didn't even know dogs had tonsils.

I guess I shouldn't complain. As long as I'm paying a vet bill, at least I'm getting my money's worth. At least tonsillitis is a real ailment, unlike the LAST time Walter had to go to the vet. It was about two months ago, and Walter had just spent three days limping and moaning around the house. I searched for burrs, broken bones, cuts, or bruises to no avail. I was heading out the front door to take Walter to the vet when my teenage daughter said, "Maybe it has something to do with the fact that Kacie's been standing on his leg."

I explained all this to the vet as he was examining my dog. When the exam was through, the good doctor gave me his recommendation: "I'd suggest you tell your five-year-old to stop standing on his leg."

"That'll be sixty dollars, please."

But I'm not complaining. Walter is worth it. He adds a lot of value to our home. I can't say how much in terms of dollars yet because I'm still researching the going rate for shed dog hair, but if there's any sort of market for this stuff at all, we could be talking really big bucks.

So I'm doing my best to keep Walter healthy. Actually,

that's my goal when it comes to the rest of my family as well. We're going into flu season, and it's time to stock up on cough syrup and decongestant.

Not to mention vitamin C, veggies, and warm mittens. After all, they say an ounce of prevention is worth a pound of cure. This is why I make my kids button up in cold weather. This is also why I tell them to "brush and floss after meals," "don't run with sharp sticks," and "please stop leaning backwards in that chair right now before you fall and break something or I walk over there and wring your neck, whichever comes first."

Walter is feeling much better, thanks for asking. In fact, I'm so stirred up by all this "ounce of prevention" stuff that I've taken a few steps to keep Walter from future ailments. He didn't seem to mind the vitamins, but trust me when I tell you he's not at all happy about the mittens.

Karen Scalf Linamen

Why did the cowboy buy a dachshund? He wanted to get a long little doggie.

Jim Kraus

The one absolutely unselfish
friend that man can have
in this selfish world, the one that
never deserts him, the one that
never proves ungrateful
or treacherous, is his dog. . .
He will kiss the hand that has
no food to offer; he will lick
the wounds and sores that come

in encounter with the roughness
of the world. . . . When all other
friends desert, he remains.

George G. Vest

FROM ROVER

Do you ever give cards and presents that come from your
pet to your family?

Barry says: A bulletin for the greeting card companies!
There are cards for just about every occasion and every situation you can think of, and pet owners love to send cards from
the family pet to dad, mom, and grandma and grandpa. In
fact, 56 percent of our pet owning families actually include a
greeting card from their pet for a birthday, anniversary,
Christmas, etc. As to gifts, 38 percent take it a step further and
buy a present for Mom, Dad, Sis and say it is from the pet.

Barry Sinrod and Marlo Mittler

JUST A WALK IN THE PARK

The zoo security guard pulled his light green Plymouth
Valiant to an abrupt halt as he approached the aquatics
section. There in the lengthening shadows of early evening
was a large male chimpanzee walking slowly toward the
back of the California sea lion exhibit. The guard had been
at the zoo long enough to recognize that this was Toto. The
zoo had eight chimpanzees in the collection. Of the eight,
Toto was the worst possible chimp to be three-quarters of a
mile from his cage. He was a former circus chimp, and in all
likelihood he had been badly abused. By human standards,
Toto was crazy, psychotic, totally unpredictable. He would be

gentle and friendly one moment and frenzied and violent the next.

The security guard rolled up his window and locked all the car doors. He reached for his walkie-talkie. He clicked it to the "on" position and it crackled to life. With his eyes fixed on the chimp that was now walking slowly toward his vehicle, he pressed the "send" button and whispered, "Sam, this is Joey... you there?"

He lifted the button and heard Sam reply, "Yeah, I'm here. What's up? Sounds like you're looking at a ghost . . . over."

"I wish I were. I'm in back of the chief keeper's shack just below the California sea lion exhibit, looking at Toto . . . over."

"Sounds like we have a problem. I'll notify the acting director and the capture team. Do your best to keep track of his whereabouts. Keep me posted. And Joey, be real careful. From what I've heard, Toto is bad news."

Joey kept track of Toto, and for whatever reason, Toto stayed near the chief's shack. He was, for all intents and purposes, lost. His zoo cage had been his territory for two years, and without help he would not be able to find his way back to it. Not knowing where he was, Toto was left with the problem of having nowhere to run. In his tangled mind he imagined he could be in enemy-occupied territory and was on the verge of emotional frenzy. He probably stayed in the area to be near the security guard who was keeping an eye on him.

Most of the capture team arrived at the same time and wisely stayed in their cars, waiting for Dr. Gale, the assistant director. Dr. Gale was an excellent animal-capture man worth waiting for, and the truth was that he would not have tolerated it any other way.

Toto was preoccupied with the sounds and smells of the immediate area and was satisfied that his company was staying in their cars. When Dr. Gale arrived, it was very dark and only the horizon gave a hint that the sun had just set for the night. The zoo's dark green shrubbery nearly absorbed Toto's silhouette, and only his occasional movement betrayed his whereabouts. Dr. Gale directed the security guard to watch Toto, then motioned for the capture team to follow him out of the area. Once out of Toto's sight, they got out of their cars and listened to Dr. Gale's plan.

"We can't dart Toto with the capture gun; it is too dark to know if we hit him. He might fall into a pool, or worst of all, we may miss and scare him so that he leaves the zoo. Then he'd need to be shot before he hurt someone in the local neighborhood. If any of you have change, give it to me." They looked at each other, wondering what Dr. Gale had up his sleeve. But they knew him well enough not to question him. The change added up to a little less than two dollars. Dr. Gale sighed as he held it in his hand. He gave Bob Spellings fifty cents of it and told him to run and get a Coke from the nearest vending machine. He told the other men to drive up to the zoo's health center, open all the doors, and wait there for him and Toto. He told them he was going to attempt to walk Toto back to his cage; but he felt the fewer animal-care staff that Toto saw, the less chance there would be of Toto's flipping out and becoming violent.

Bob Spelling returned with the Coke and handed it to Dr. Gale who took a sip, and smiled a "wish-me-luck" smile. He waited for the men to clear the area, then walked slowly toward Toto. When he was nearing the escaped chimp he could see that Toto was a bit apprehensive, and even in the dark he could see that Toto was beginning to stand; his hair was on end, and he looked as if he were about to charge.

Dr. Gale spoke softly, "You want something to drink, Toto?" Toto settled down and walked slowly forward and looked briefly at the cup and then into Dr. Gale's eyes. He reached for the man's hand and pulled it and the cup to his mouth and moaned contentedly. He poured most of the cup into his mouth. Dr. Gale was wishing the zoo served larger Cokes, because his plan was to lure him from vending machine to vending machine until they reached Toto's cage.

But if Toto were going to finish everything so quickly, he might not follow to the next reward. Even worse, he might want more, and there would be no more to give him. It never took much to disturb Toto, and that was the last thing Dr. Gale wanted to happen alone in the dark in the middle of the zoo. He was already questioning the wisdom of his own plan and looked around to see if any of the men were still nearby to suggest Plan B. But he was alone. He wasn't really alone; there was a psychotic former circus chimp standing at his side drinking the last drop of Coke out of a cup that seemed smaller than ever.

Dr. Gale saw the chief keeper's building and concluded that he might buy some time if he could lock Toto in the building. So he offered Toto his hand, and Toto took it—something he would have done as a young chimp but may not do for long as an old chimp who was six times as strong as the man who was leading him. Dr. Gale removed his keys from his pocket and unlocked the chief keeper's office. He walked into the dark office, hoping Toto would follow. He did. It was darker inside than out and Dr. Gale waited until he was sure Toto was fully inside.

Then Dr. Gale made a quick move and slipped out the door as quickly as he could. He slammed the door and locked it. His heart was pounding and beads of perspiration were forming on his forehead. He wiped it with his handkerchief and walked on his tiptoes to see if Toto was calmly inside. He shaded his eyes from the glare of the street light that created reflections on the window and stared into the darkness of the office. He strained his eyes to see Toto, but could not locate the chimp. He felt a hand on his shoulder and slowly turned to find himself face to face with a disturbed Toto. In a mimicking fashion, Toto was also shielding his eyes from the reflection as he, too, stared into the darkness, trying to discover what had frightened the doctor out of the office.

"Let's go home, Toto," said the doctor, resigned to the first plan. Toto followed him to the next vending machine where he purchased a small box of Good and Plenty candies. Toto enjoyed them immensely, but he would stop, sit down, and suck on them, so progress was somewhat impeded. Dr. Gale was limited to one more purchase, and he was not even half way to the health center. The wizened vet noticed a drinking fountain and turned the handle to show Toto that he could get a drink. Toto drank copious drafts of water and was captured by the novelty of the drinking device.

A lion roared from its night quarters. Toto stood straight up and rocked back and forth as if he were going to begin an aggressive display. He ran toward the lion and screamed one loud scream as a warning to his unseen enemy. Then he looked back at Dr. Gale as if to say, "Well, I guess that takes care of that." Dr. Gale praised him in a soft voice and rewarded him with a Good and Plenty.

The Good and Plenty ran out, so he made one last purchase. A Payday candy bar slid out of the vending machine. Toto watched with interest as its wrapper was peeled away and a small piece was handed to him. Dr. Gale walked faster now, knowing he was on borrowed time. Toto grunted a "wait for me" sound and ran on all fours to catch up. The Payday was clearly a favorite choice. The chimp tugged at his benefactor's pant leg for another piece. Progress was now at a sufficient pace, and it looked as though they might make it to the health center after all.

As they rounded the corner at the mountain zebra exhibit, a terror-filled event took place. Ed Alonzo, the principal keeper, was waiting fifty yards away under a street light, monitoring the doctor's journey. If Dr. Gale got in trouble, Ed wanted to be there to help. But now Ed was in trouble. When Toto saw Ed under the street light, he stood up and hooted. He bolted away from Dr. Gale and ran at full speed toward the frozen principal keeper. Toto had injured others, and Ed fully expected to be bitten and beaten within an inch of his life, so he braced himself for the attack.

Toto looked menacing as he charged closer and closer. Ed swallowed and prepared himself for the awesome impact he was about to experience. At the last possible second, Toto pulled up short and stood up in front of Ed to greet him. Ed had been his keeper a few years before, and Toto was merely saying hello with a great deal of enthusiasm. Seeing a person that Toto remembered fondly had thoroughly piqued his interest. He had grown tired of the night's adventure, and Ed probably represented care and security. Toto reached for Ed's hand, which was shaking noticeably from the massive dose of adrenalin which had just been released into his system. The baton had been handed to Ed, so the last hundred yards were his to accomplish.

He and Toto walked up a narrow overgrown path, and when they reached the top, they could see the health center in full view. Toto released Ed's hand and again ran full speed until he had entered the health center's surgery door. He walked down the well-lighted hallway into the cage room and stood peering through the open door of his cage as if he were trying to make up his mind, "Shall I go in, or shall I stay out?" It was at this point that Bill Dickman, a brave and foolish keeper, ran full swing into Toto, bumping him into his cage and slamming the door behind him. Toto hooted his displeasure, but he decided to be forgiving because he was so glad to be home.

Gary Richmond

···

The only creature that can keep his feet on the ground while his head is in the clouds is the giraffe.

···

Animals

Q. What kind of snack do little monkeys have with their milk?

A. Chocolate chimp cookies.

Q. What do you get when you cross a pig and a centipede?

A. Bacon and legs.

Q. What's a cat's favorite breakfast?

A. Mice Krispies

Q. What do whales like to chew?

A. Blubber gum.

Q. How does a lion like his steak?

A. Medium roar.

Q. What do frogs eat with their hamburgers?

A. French flies.

Q. What do cats like on their hot dogs?

A. Mouse-tard.

Q. What is a little dog's favorite drink?

A. Pupsi-cola.

Funny Bone

* * *

Pets are people too. If you don't believe it, just try sitting in their favorite chair!

Mary Hollingsworth

**"I think it's one of those housing bubbles
you hear them talk about on the news."**

BEET PULP SAFETY WARNING
(AKA THE FAMOUS SQUIRREL STORY)

People into equine nutrition are notorious for spending their time doing the strangest things. Normal horse people have nightmares about finding themselves riding in the World Equestrian Games stark naked past the ESPN cameras. Nutrition-oriented horse people instead fret over whether their carefully thought-out recommendations will make the difference between Muffy the Superhorse winning his next competition in fame and glory, or falling into a dead faint somewhere between being saddled and the starting line.

In the end, the finer points of nutrition often make zero difference, however, because you generally find out that: a) Muffy won't even touch your carefully crafted ration, much preferring to eat his bedding, the vet's fingers, and anything from the Taco Bell menu; or b) the moment you finish calculating the perfect equine ration featuring Aunt Tilly's Super Horsey Hum Yums, the feed company goes out of business or is indicted on environmental pollution charges; or c) it's all irrelevant, anyway, because the barn manager's favorite phrase is, "Well, my pa always fed horses this way and we hardly ever lose more than two or three a month to botulism," steadfastly refusing to feed anything at all other than His Very Own Secret Recipe, featuring lawn clippings, beer, and something that smells a lot like roadkill.

However, every now and then, you stumble across a feed that horses actually like (at least, after that initial suspicious, "You're trying to poison me, aren't you?" look), is nutritious, cheap and still obscure and mysterious enough that people feel like they're really on the cutting edge in feeding it to Muffy. Beet pulp is like that, and for a long time I thought the only disadvantage to it was the minor inconvenience of having to soak it in generous amounts of water before feeding. Some folks skip that part, but others revel in it, making sure everyone else in the barn knows just how conscientious and detail-minded they are about Muffy's nutritional well-being.

Eventually I knew the true downside to beet pulp would show up, and thought it only fair that I pass it along with fair warning.

This afternoon I decided to bring some beet pulp pellets into the house to soak, because I wanted to get an idea of exactly how much they expanded in volume during the soaking process. Academic types are like that, pathetically easy to amuse and desperately in need of professional help. I knew they expanded quite a bit, because the first time I'd innocently added water to a five-pound bucket of beet pulp, I'd come back later to find my feed room practically awash in beet pulp, providing a breakfast that every horse within a five mile radius still remembers with fond nostalgia. So in the interest of scientific curiosity, I trundled in a bucket, added about three or four pounds of beet pulp, and plenty of water, and set it in the living room to do its thing. No problem. Hey presto, research in action.

Coincidentally, in our ongoing quest to turn this house into Noah's Ark, we have not only four horses, three dogs, four neurotic cats, a sulfur-crested cockatoo, and assorted toads, we also have William. William is a fox squirrel who absent-mindedly fell out of his tree as a blind and hairless baby two years ago and whom the vet promptly handed off to the only person he knew idiotic enough to traipse around with a baby squirrel and a bottle of milk replacer tucked in her bookbag. Actually the trick wasn't in keeping such a tiny creature warm, fed, and clean—it was keeping a straight face and looking as mystified as everyone else when William woke up hungry and started pipping for his bottle like a very small, slightly muffled alarm clock.

Invariably, this usually occurred standing in line at the grocery store checkout, in an overcrowded elevator, or on one memorable occasion, taking a final exam in biochemistry. Being no dummy, William knew a sucker when he saw one and has happily been an urban squirrel ever since.

And for those of you that think a squirrel's place is in the wild, don't think we didn't try that . . . his first Christmas, we thought we'd give him his first lesson in being wild by letting him practice his climbing skills in the undecorated Christmas tree. His reaction was to shriek in horror, scoot frantically across the floor and go try to hide underneath the nearest border collie. Since then, the only way he will allow himself to be taken outside is hiding inside Mummy's shirt and peering suspiciously out at the sinister world.

So much for the Yuletide version of *Born Free.* So secure is William about his karmic niche in the universe that on more than one occasion, I've caught him sitting on his fat, smug little bottom, making faces out the window at our local red-tailed hawk—like as not cheerfully clutching a piece of mango in a sticky paw while his would-be predator glares back in hunger and frustration.

Anyway, when I set out the bucket of beet pulp, I may have underestimated the lengths that an enthusiastic squirrel will go to in order to stash all available food items in new and unusual hiding spots. I thought letting William out of his cage as usual and giving him a handful of almonds to go happily

cram under cushions and into sleeping dogs' ears was sufficient entertainment for the afternoon. After all, when I left, he
was gleefully chortling and gloating over his pile of treasure,
making sure the cockatoo saw them so he could tell her I have
almonds and you don't. So much for foolish optimism.

Apparently when the almond supply ran out, beet pulp
pellets became fair game and I can only imagine the little rat
finding that great big bucket and swooning with the possibilities of being able to hide away such a bountiful and God-
given largesse. The problem isn't quite so much that I now
have a generous supply of beet pulp pellets cleverly tucked
away in every corner of my house, it's that as far as I can tell,
the soaking-expanding-and-falling-apart process seems to be
somewhat like nuclear fission. Once the reaction gets rolling,
no force on earth is going to stop it.

So when I come back from the grocery store, not only do I
find an exhausted but fulfilled squirrel snoozing happily up
on the cat tree, I find that my house smells a lot like a
Jamaican feed mill and virtually every orifice is crammed full
of soggy beet pulp. This includes the bathroom sink drains,
every last crevice of the fish tank filter, deep in the toes of
every shoe in the closet and even my undie drawer, in the
kitty box (much to the cats' horror). Not to mention that in
enthusiastically stuffing beet pulp into the little box of live
crickets destined for the toad's dinner, William managed to
open it up and free several hundred former captives into the
living room. It's not that I mind crickets springing to and fro,
it's just that it sounds a lot like an evening in the Amazon
Rain Forest in here. The cats, on the other hand have never
had such a marvelous time steeplechasing after stray crickets
back and forth over the furniture, crunching up the spoils of
the hunt (which wouldn't be so bad if they would just chew
with their mouths closed), and sicking up the more indi-
gestible parts onto the rug.

I simply can't WAIT to turn on the furnace and find out

what toasting beet pulp smells like. The good news is that in case of siege, I have enough carbohydrates hidden in my walls and under the furniture to survive for years. The bad news is that as soon as I try to remove any of this stash, I get a hysterical squirrel clinging to my pant leg, tearfully shrieking that I'm ruining all his hard work and now he's going to starve this winter. This is despite the fact that William is spoiled utterly rotten, knows how to open the macadamia nut can all by himself, and has enough of a tummy to have earned him the unfortunate nickname Buddha Belly.

In case anyone was losing sleep wondering just how much final product you get after soaking three pounds of beet pulp, the answer is a house full. I'd write this new data up and submit it as a case study paper to the nutrition and physiology society, but I suspect the practical applications may be limited.

Off to go empty the Shop-Vac. Again.

Susan Evans Garlinghouse

> So in case anyone was . . . wondering just how much final product you get after soaking three pounds of beet pulp, the answer is a house full.

....

UCLA football coach Pepper Rodgers was in the middle of a terrible season. It even got so bad that it upset his home life. He recalls, "My dog was my only friend. I told my wife that a man needs at least two friends, and she bought me another dog."

Michael Hodgin

....

A PET DILEMMA FOR THE MODERN FAMILY

She was looking at me so sadly. She leaned forward with her head dropped down, forcing her eyes to roll up towards her forehead to see me. I had only just noticed her staring at me. I had been peering into my computer screen for several hours now. I puzzled over what might be making her so sad and then, it dawned on me.

Dallas, our family dog, had gone from room to room, visiting each family member. We were each staring into our computer screens. It was only in the past month or so that my youngest daughter had gotten her own computer. Now, each family member had a computer. My daughter was online all the time now, instant messaging her friends. Before this computer arrived, there was always someone without their hands on a keyboard, free to play with the dog, or at least be active in some way, and the dog would follow that person around.

I wondered what the dog must think of us. I had been motionless for quite a bit, just staring at the document displayed on the monitor, lost in thought. When Dallas visited my daughter, she was in another room, banging keys on the keyboard, gossiping with several friends simultaneously via the message service. The computer was continually blaring that odd jingle noise that occurs every time a message comes in. What could the dog possibly make of my daughter's continuous keyboarding and rapt attention to her screen?

The dog had visited my wife as well. She was working in the dining room, preparing the next day's lesson plan on her laptop. All the dog knows is that each of us was sitting, engaged in the computer screen, barely moving except for some minor keyboarding and mouse movements. I don't know whether the dog has the intelligence to realize how computers have changed our lives over the past couple years, as we acquired more of them and one by one we became lost in their presence.

Dallas probably remembers she used to get more attention even if she didn't recognize the trend of each new computer's arrival absorbing another family member. So I understood now why she stared at me. The family which she thought of as her "pack" and her home, have been transformed into some kind of wax museum with slow moving, nearly frozen images of her packmates. Most importantly, wax replicas or not, she was being ignored by us for the better part of each day. Maybe she thought she had done something wrong and was being punished.

I launched into problem solving. How to fix this unhappy dog syndrome? To be honest my first thought was to replace the dog with a virtual pet. No more walking the dog in bad weather and expensive dog food, just a cartoon figure intruding onto my screen from time to time, making me acknowledge it by mousing over it or perhaps typing "biscuit" or some such. Perhaps I could command it to go bother my daughter and it would leave my screen and jump via the Internet to hers. That would more or less emulate what I often suggest to Dallas.

To be honest my first thought was to replace the dog with a virtual pet.

As appealing as a computer pet sounded to me, I knew my daughter wouldn't let me get rid of Dallas. I needed an alternative. How else to fix a dog forlorn by its computer-networked family? Of course! Solution #2: I'll get the dog a computer! I imagined there must be some programs that would entertain a dog. Heck, a few occasional virtual squirrels and a virtual postman for real excitement would probably do.

I wondered whether Dallas's drool would damage the keyboard.

Meanwhile, Dallas was still staring sadly at me, although now I was absent-mindedly staring back at her. It finally occurred to me that staring at the computer all day and seriously considering either virtual pets or computers for dogs, were reasons enough to take a break. I got up and took Dallas outside for a walk. She was now thrilled, her tail wagging excitedly, as we greeted our neighbors out with their pets. As we walked, I began mentally picturing buddy icons for Dallas's friends. . . .

Tex Texin

•••

If toast always lands butter-side down, and cats always land on their feet, what happens if you strap toast on the back of a cat and drop it?

Steven Wright

•••

A DOG'S PLEA

Treat me kindly, my beloved friend, for no heart in all the world is more grateful for kindness than the loving heart of me.

Do not break my spirit with a stick, for though I might lick your hand between blows, your patience and understanding will more quickly teach me the things you would have me learn.

Speak to me often, for your voice is the world's sweetest music, as you must know by the fierce wagging of my tail when your footstep falls upon my waiting ear.

Please take me inside when it is cold and wet, for I am a domesticated animal, no longer accustomed to bitter elements. I ask no greater glory than the privilege of sitting at your feet beside the hearth.

Keep my pan filled with fresh water, for I cannot tell you when I suffer thirst.

Feed me clean food that I may stay well, to romp and play and do your bidding, to walk by your side, and stand ready, willing and able to protect you with my life, should your life be in danger.

And, my friend, when I am very old, and I no longer enjoy good health, hearing and sight, do not make heroic efforts to keep me going. I am not having any fun. Please see that my trusting life is taken gently. I shall leave this earth knowing with the last breath I draw that my fate was always safest in your hands.

Author unknown

Heaven will not ever heaven be
Unless my pet is there to welcome me.

EPITAPH IN A PET CEMETERY

Acknowledgments

All material that originally appeared in *Daily Guideposts* and *Guideposts* magazine is reprinted with permission. Copyright ©1983–2005 by Guideposts, Carmel, New York 10512. All rights reserved.

Armstrong, Patti. "Temporary Insanity." Used by permission.

Berk, Suzanne. "Sammie and Sugar." © 2006. Used by permission. Visit www.petfinder.com to find out how to adopt rescued dogs and cats.

The Best of Uncle John's Bathroom Reader. Ashland, OR: Bathroom Readers Press, 1995. www.bathroomreader.com.

Bigger, Margaret G. *Kitties and All That Litter.* Charlotte, NC: A. Borough Books, 1999.

Bolton, Martha. *Who Put the Pizza in the VCR?* Ventura, CA: Vine Books, 1996. Used by permission of author.

Bohrer, Walt and Ann. "This is Your Captain Speaking," *Daily Telegraph*, Sept. 25, 1985.

Bonham, Tal D. *The Treasury of Clean Jokes*. Nashville, TN: Broadman & Holman, 1997.

Breedlove, Connie Macsas. *A Funny Thing Happened on the Way to Heaven*. Grand Rapids, MI: Zondervan, 1996.

Bricklin, Mark. *Pets' Letters to God*. New York: Rodale, 1999.

Brownlow, Leroy. *Let's Laugh a Little*. Fort Worth, TX: Brownlow, 1993. Used by permission.

Coleman, Britta. "Zorro." Used by permission. Britta Coleman (www.brittacoleman.com) is an award-winning author, journalist, and inspirational speaker. Her debut novel, *Potter Springs*, won the Lone Star Scribe Award, and her "Practically Parenting" column is published as a regular newspaper feature. Britta lives in Fort Worth, TX with her husband, two children, and two Chihuahuas.

Davis, Lise Ann. "Things I Learned from my Dog." Used by permission.

Decker, David. "Chicken Fishin'." Found on http://libjohnbrown.blogspot.com.

Dickson, Paul. *The Official Rules at Home*. New York: Walker and Company, 1996.

Fillion, Jo-Ann Burke. "Ferrets for the Fun of It." Used by permission.

Garlinghouse, Susan Evans. "Beet Pulp Safety Warning." © 1997. Found on http://shady-acres.com/susan/squirrel.shtml.

Gaspirtz, Oliver. *A Treasury of Pet Humor*. Springfield, IL: Lincoln-Herndon Press, 1999.

Gordon, Arthur. *A Touch of Wonder*. Grand Rapids, MI: Fleming H. Revell, a division of Baker Publishing Group, 1974.

Grizzard, Louis. *Chili Dawgs Always Bark at Night*. New York: Villard, a division of Random House, 1989.

Hale, Leon. *Turn South at the Second Bridge*. New York: Doubleday, 1965. www.leonhale.com.

Taken from *1001 Humorous Illustrations for Public Speaking* by Michael Hodgin. Copyright ©1994 by Michael Hodgin. Used by permission of The Zondervan Corporation.

Hogan, Rhonda. "Fur People." Used by permission of Creative Solutions, Arlington, TX.

Hollingsworth, Mary. "The Tummy Timer." Administered by Shady Oaks Studio, 1507 Shirley Way, Bedford, TX 76022. Used by permission.

———. *Polka Dots, Stripes, Humps 'n' Hatracks*. © 1990. Administered by Shady Oaks Studio, 1507 Shirley Way, Bedford, TX 76022. Used by permission.

———."Crackerjack." Administered by Shady Oaks Studio, 1507 Shirley Way, Bedford, TX 76022. Used by permission.

Kraus, James. *Bloopers, Blunders, Quips, Jokes, and Quotes*. Wheaton, IL: Tyndale, 2005. Used by permission.

Linamen, Karen Scalf. *Welcome to the Funny Farm*. Grand Rapids, MI: Fleming Revell, a division of Baker Publishing Group, 2001.

Taken from *Extravagant Grace* by Patsy Clairmont, Barbara E. Johnson, Meberg, Marilyn, Luci Swindoll, Sheila Walsh, and Thelma Wells. Copyright © 2000 by Women of Faith, Inc. Used by permission of The Zondervan Corporation.

Mickle, Shelley Fraser. *Kids are Gone, The Dog is Depressed & Mom's on the Loose*. Gainesville, FL: Alachua Press, 2000. Used by permission.

Moss, Sheila. "Attack of the Butterfly." Used by permission. Sheila Moss is a self-syndicated humor columnist from Tennessee. She is best known as an Internet columnist, but also has been published in book anthologies, magazines, and newspapers. www.humorcolumnist.com

———. "A Boy's First Frog." Used by permission. Sheila Moss is a self-syndicated humor columnist from Tennessee. She is best known as an Internet columnist, but also has been published in book anthologies, magazines, and newspapers. www.humorcolumnist.com.

———. "Invisible Cat." Used by permission. Sheila Moss is a self-syndicated humor columnist from Tennessee. She is best known as an Internet columnist, but also has been published in book anthologies, magazines, and newspapers. www.humorcolumnist.com.

Phillips, Cathy Lee. *Gutsy Little Flower.* Canton, GA: Patchwork Press, 2001. Used by permission. www.cathyleephillips.com.

———. "Ashley at the Gate." Used by permission. www.cathyleephillips.com.

Prairie Home Companion. *Pretty Good Joke Book.* Minneapolis, MN: Highbridge Company, 2003.

Reprinted with the permission of Simon & Schuster. Adult Publishing Group from *It's Always Something* by Gilda Radner. Copyright ©1989 by Gilda Radner.

Renner, Kathryn. "Trading Spaces with the Dog." *Better Homes and Garden,* April 2006, 280.

Richmond, Gary. *A View from the Zoo.* Nashville: W Publishing Group, 1987. More of Gary's stories can be found in *A New View from the Zoo* published by DMJ Media Group.

———. *Please Don't Feed the Bears*. Nashville: W. Publishing Group, 1990. More of Gary's stories can be found in *A New View from the Zoo* published by DMJ Media Group.

Sinrod, Barry and Marlo Mittler. *Do You Treat Your Pet As If It Were Your Child?* New York: Select Books, 2002.

Stibbe, Mark and J. John. *A Bucket of Surprises*. Oxford, UK: Monarch, 2002.

Texin, Tex. "A Pet Dilemma for the Modern Family." © 2002 Tex Texin. All rights reserved. Originally published at: http://www.i18nguy.com/humor/petdilemma.html.

Torrey, Isabel Wolseley. "Dogs, People Much Alike." Used by permission.

———. "Why Not Pet Exemptions?" Used by permission.

Walker, Laura Jensen. *Through the Rocky Road and into the Rainbow Sherbet*. Grand Rapids, MI: Fleming Revell, a division of Baker Book House, 2002.

Wells, Carol. "The Garbage Disposal." Carol A. Wells is the mother of five children and a freelance writer. She is originally from central Indiana, lived briefly in southern New Jersey, and currently resides in the western Pennsylvania area. More stories about Carol's family located at www.humorisrelative.com that features non-fiction humorous stories about family, contributed by a variety of writers and columnists.

Wright, Rusty and Linda Raney. *500 Clean Jokes and Humorous Stories* published by Barbour Publishing, Inc. Uhrichsville, OH: Barbour, 1985. Used by permission.

A Note from the Editors

This original book was created by the Books and Inspirational Media Division of Guideposts, the world's leading inspirational publisher. Founded in 1945 by Dr. Norman Vincent Peale and his wife Ruth Stafford Peale, Guideposts helps people from all walks of life achieve their maximum personal and spiritual potential. Guideposts is committed to communicating positive, faith-filled principles for people everywhere to use in successful daily living.

Other publications include award-winning magazines like *Guideposts, Angels on Earth, Sweet 16,* and *Positive Thinking,* best-selling books, and outreach services that demonstrate what can happen when faith and positive thinking are applied to day-to-day life.

For more information, visit us online at www.guideposts.org, call (800) 431-2344, or write Guideposts, 39 Seminary Hill Road, Carmel, New York 10512.